Goldsmiths UNIVERSITY OF LONDON

Centre for Public and Voluntary Sector Development

Grants from Europe

Ann Davison read politics at the University of Southampton. She then worked for *Which?* magazine, and later became secretary of the Consumers in the European Community Group (CECG), which represents voluntary and professional organisations with consumer interests in EC issues.

Her special concerns are agriculture, the environment and world development issues and she was national chair of the World Development Movement. Ann represents consumers nationally, at European level and internationally on these subjects and is helping to launch 'development-friendly' labelling in Britain.

She works from her home in Surrey where she lives with her husband, Robert Jenkins, and their three young children. In her spare time she chairs the Leatherhead World Development Group and her local church's Social Concern Committee.

NCVO – voice of the voluntary sector

NCVO champions the cause of the voluntary sector. It believes that the voluntary sector enriches society and needs to be promoted and supported. It works to improve its effectiveness, identify unmet needs and encourage initiatives to meet them.

Established in 1919 as the representative body for the voluntary sector in England, NCVO now gives voice to some 600 national organisations – from large 'household name' charities to small self-help groups involved in all areas of voluntary and social action. It is also in touch with thousands of other voluntary bodies and groups, and has close links with government departments, local authorities, the European Community and the business sector.

Grants from Europe

How to Get Money and Influence Policy

Seventh Edition

Written for Erica by
Ann Davison

NCVO Publications

Published by
NCVO Publications
(incorporating Bedford Square Press)
imprint of the
National Council for Voluntary
Organisations
Regent's Wharf, 8 All Saints Street,
London N1 9RL

First published 1984
Second edition 1985
Third edition 1986
Fourth edition 1988
Fifth edition 1989
Reprinted 1990
Sixth edition 1990
Reprinted 1991

Typeset by GCS, Leighton Buzzard,
Bedfordshire
Printed in Great Britain by
The Lavenham Press Limited, Suffolk

A catalogue record for this book is
available from the British Library.

ISBN 0 7199 1382 9

Contents

Foreword to the Seventh Edition

This is the seventh edition in nine years of *Grants from Europe*, and we hope that its readers will find it as useful as they have found its predecessors. There have been considerable changes in Brussels and a new guide is needed to help us find our way among them.

The Berlaymont, home of the EC Commission, is no longer in use (because of asbestos in its construction) and the civil servants have been dispersed to new addresses. Telephone numbers have changed. Important fax numbers have been added. There have been staff changes. Policies have changed – usually to expand – or have acquired a different emphasis. The Community has decided to call itself the EC (European Community) instead of the European Economic Community (EEC). All of this you will find in the current edition, documented as usefully as we know how.

There are things, however, that don't change. The Brussels bureaucracy is really quite small – about the same number of officials for the 12 Member States as are needed for the Scottish Office. So it is quite manageable. The civil servants are approachable – more so, probably, than Whitehall. Most of them, including the switchboard operators, speak English, so that conversation – for us, at any rate – is easy. Brussels, once you get to know it, has its beauties. And you would have to try very hard to get a bad meal there.

But many of the procedures are strange to us. If we want to influence the Community with our ideas, if we want to get the financial help we are entitled to with our work, we need to become familiar with them. The official language, cluttered with initials, has to be learnt. And the policies, rooted in history, have to be understood.

ERICA hopes that this edition of *Grants from Europe* will help, as we know the others have done.

Eirlys Roberts

Chairman
ERICA
(European Research into Consumer Affairs)
8 Lloyd Square
London WC1X 9BA
Tel: 071-837 2492
Fax: 071-482 6376

Acknowledgements

We should like to thank the Charities Aid Foundation for its contribution towards originating this project. We should also like to thank the NGDO-EC Liaison Committee; the European Commission; the UK Department of Trade and Industry; Bill Seary, who was co-author of the sixth edition; CECG; ECAS; Mary Williams; Clive Gardner and many others for their generous help in preparing this guide. Any errors or omissions are the author's alone.

Abbreviations

ACP	African, Caribbean and Pacific
ARION	EC programme financing study trips for teachers in the various Community countries
BEUC	European Bureau of Consumer Unions
BRIDGE	Biotechnology Research for Innovation, Development and Growth in Europe
CAP	Common Agricultural Policy
CBI	Confederation of British Industry
CECG	Consumers in the European Community Group
CEDAG	European Council of Voluntary Organisations
CEDEFOP	European Centre for the Development of Vocational Training
CEE	Centre for European Education
COFACE	Confederation of Family Organisations in the European Communities
COMETT	Co-operation between Universities and Enterprises on Training in the Field of Technology
COREPER	Committee of Permanent Representatives
COST	European Co-operation in Science and Technology
CREW	Centre for Research on European Women
CSFs	Community Support Frameworks
DE	Department of Employment
DES	Department of Education and Science
DG V	Directorate-General Five of the EC Commission
DoE	Department of the Environment
EBIS	European Biotechnology Information Service
ECAS	Euro Citizen Action Service
ECSC	European Coal and Steel Communities
ECU	European Currency Unit

ECWS	European Centre for Work and Society
EDF	European Development Fund
EEB	European Environmental Bureau
EEIG	European Economic Interest Grouping
EFTA	European Free Trade Association
EIB	European Investment Bank
ENVIREG	Programme organising the fight against pollution in coastal areas
ERASMUS	European Community Action Scheme for the Mobility of University Students
ERDF	European Regional Development Fund
ERICA	European Research into Consumer Affairs
ERM	Exchange Rate Mechanism
ESA	Environmentally Sensitive Area
ESC	Economic and Social Committee
ESF	European Social Fund
ETUC	European Trades Union Confederation
EUCREA	Organisation linking national bodies in stimulating artistic creativity among people with disabilities
EURATOM	European Atomic Energy Community
EUROPOL	Future European police organisation, aimed primarily at co-ordinating the struggle against drug traffic
EURYDICE	Education Information Network in the European Community
FEEE	Foundation for Environmental Education in Europe
FORCE	Programme for company-based continuing vocational training
HANDYNET	Computerised information system covering questions concerning people with disabilities in the EC
HELIOS	Community programme for the disabled
HORIZON	Aid programme financing vocational training for handicapped people
IRIS	EC network of vocational training programmes for women
LEADER	Liaison between actions for the development of the rural economy
LEDA	Local Employment Development Action Programme
LINGUA	A programme to promote foreign language teaching
LIFE	Financial instrument for the environment
MAFF	Ministry of Agriculture, Fisheries and Food
MEP	Member of the European Parliament
NCI	New Community Instrument
NCVO	National Council for Voluntary Organisations
NGO	non-governmental organisation

NGDO	non-governmental development organisation
OJ	Official Journal of the European Communities
PETRA	EC programme to help vocational training projects for 16 to 27 year olds
PHARE	Assistance programmes for the Central and Eastern European Countries
SCVO	Scottish Council for Voluntary Organisations
STEP	Science and Technology for Environment and Protection
SYSDEM	System of Documentation on Employment
TIDE	Technology for the Integration of the Disabled and Elderly
TUC	Trades Union Congress
UKREP	UK Permanent Representation
UNICE	Union of the Industries of the European Communities
WCVA	Wales Council for Voluntary Action

1 *Introduction*

The decisions of the European Community affect you. They affect you at work; they affect you at home. If you work for an interest group, you may well find the Community's 'civil service', the Commission, an unexpected ally. You need to know how the Community works, what funds it has available for private organisations, what decisions it makes and how you can influence them. This handbook, aimed particularly at voluntary organisations, but also at trade unions, local authorities, small businesses, schools and academics, will tell you.

The European Community has fingers in many pies. It helps to determine United Kingdom policies on employment, trade, energy, world develoment, competition, regional development, industry and the economy. Its interests include working conditions, the needs of poor people, people with disabilities, women, young people, migrant workers, immigrants, consumers and the environment. It is involved in culture, education, health and human rights issues.

The first two chapters of this book describe the structures and procedures of the European Community, give a brief analysis of the centres of influence and set out some of the ground rules for bringing influence to bear. Chapters 3 to 13 work through the subjects of greatest interest to voluntary organisations, outlining the Community's involvement and giving the detail you need to make your own approaches. Chapter 14 will help to smooth the practical arrangements for any trips to Brussels you may need in order to make your own approaches.

1.1 What is the European Community?

In fact, there are three communities: the European Economic Community (the 'Common Market') established in 1958; the European Atomic Energy Community (Euratom), also established in 1958, and the European Coal and

1

Steel Community, established in 1952. In 1967 the communities merged their institutional structures. Each retains its integrity under international law but in practice they work together. The Commission administers all three as if they were one.

In 1958 there were six member states: Belgium, West Germany, France, Italy, Luxembourg and the Netherlands. They were joined in 1973 by Denmark, Ireland and the United Kingdom, in 1981 by Greece, in 1986 by Portugal and Spain and in 1991 by East Germany, when it re-united with West Germany. Formal applications for membership have been received from Austria, Switzerland, Finland, Norway and Sweden (all members of EFTA) as well as Cyprus, Malta and Turkey (whose applications are more controversial). The target date for accession of the EFTA countries is 1 January 1995. Other countries which have announced their intention of joining the Community, or are discussing the possibility, are Iceland, Liechtenstein, the Czech and Slovak repubics, Poland, Hungary, Estonia, Latvia, Lithuania, Bulgaria, Rumania and Albania.

1.2 The institutions

Community policies and legislation are based on the founding treaties (one for each community), as amended by subsequent treaties such as the Single European Act (1987) and the Maastricht Treaty.

1.2.1 The Commission

When people talk about 'Brussels', they are normally referring to the Commission. Its headquarters is scattered around the area of Brussels near the Berlaymont, which is the star-shaped building frequently seen on television. The Commission is the only institution with the right to initiate proposals for legislation, budgets and programmes of work. It is responsible for administering agreed programmes. It represents the Community as a whole in international discussions. It is the duty of the Commission to monitor the way in which the founding treaties and subsequent legislation are observed by the member states. If necessary, it can take cases before the European Court of Justice for a final decision on the legality of any particular action.

In one sense the 'Commission' is composed of 17 commissioners. Commissioners are supposed to be appointed by the Council of Ministers (see ss 1.2.4) on the recommendation of national governments (two from each large country; one from small ones). In practice governments put forward only one name for each place and the Council rubber-stamps this list. The President of the Commission is one of the 17. He or she is nominated by the member states before any of the others. It is now the practice for the views of the Parliament to be invited on the proposed nomination. Commissioners normally come from a background of national politics, and when a country has two places it will normally nominate people from different parties. These people are collectively subjected to a Parliamentary vote of approval and then take an oath to serve the Community as a whole, without favour to their own country. The commissioners take their decisions collectively but, as in a national government, each commissioner has a portfolio of topics on which he or she is responsible for proposals and for the administration of programmes of work. Commissioners have had a four-year, renewable, term of office but the present commissioners are in their posts for only two years, from January 1993 to the end of 1994. Thereafter, the terms will last for five years to run parallel to those of the European Parliament.

In a wider, and more common, sense the 'Commission' is the bureaucracy which supports the commissioners. This bureaucracy is headed by the directors general of which there are 23 at present. Each has a directorate-general responsible to them which is known by a number (usually written in roman numerals). Thus, the one which is responsible for agriculture is known as DG VI. The work of the directorates-general is co-ordinated by the Secretary General of the Commission. Some commissioners have more than one director general reporting to them. It is also possible, though not common, for a director general to report to different commissioners for different parts of his or her work.

It is the bureaucracy that enables the Commission to carry out its functions. The people who staff it draft proposed legislation, develop ideas for new areas of work, administer agreed programmes and monitor the compliance of member states with Community legislation. There are about 13,000 officials, which to a voluntary organisation may sound a great number, but in fact this is comparable in size to the Scottish Office. In the case of the Commission, however, a third of the staff are employed on the translation and interpretation required as a consequence of the Community having nine working languages.

Language is a significant factor in the administration of the European Community. It introduces not only expense but also considerable delays, for example, between a decision being taken and final agreement on the nine texts so that publication can take place. Language misunderstandings can cause problems, and language is one of the reasons why correspondence with the Commission is normally slow and stilted. Voluntary organisations (notably ERICA and CECG) are encouraging the EC to use plainer language which should help. The Commission uses acronyms to name its programmes (ERASMUS for exchanges at the level of tertiary education and IRIS for the network of women's employment projects, to give but two examples) partly to avoid translation.

President: Jacques Delors:
Secretariat General; Forward Research Unit; General Inspectorate of Services; Legal Service; Monetary Affairs; Spokesman Service; Common 'Conference Interpreting' Service; Security Office

Henning Christophersen:
Economic and Financial Affairs; Monetary Affairs (with President Delors); Credit and Investments; Statistical Office

Manuel Marin:
Co-operation and Development – economic co-operation relations with the countries of the Southern Mediterranean, Middle East, Near East, Latin America and Asia; Lomé Convention; European Emergency Humanitarian Aid Office

Martin Bangemann:
Industrial Affairs; Information Technologies and Telecommunications

Sir Leon Brittan:
External Economic Affairs (North America, Japan, China, Community of Independent States, Europe, including Central and Eastern Europe); Commercial Policy

Abel Matutes:
Energy and Euratom Supply Agency; Transport

Peter Schmidhuber:
Budgets; Financial Control; Anti-fraud; Cohesion Fund – co-ordination and management

Christiane Scrivener:
Customs and Indirect Taxation; Direct Taxation; Consumer Policy

Bruce Millan:
Regional Policy; Relations with the Committee of Regions

Karel Van Miert:
Competition Policy; Personnel and Administration Policy; Translation and Computer Technology

Hans van den Broek:
External Political Relations; Common External and Security Policy; Enlargement Negotiations (Task Force)

Joao Pinheiro:
Relations with European Parliament; Relations with the Member States on matters of Transparency, Communication and Information; Culture and Audiovisual; Office for Publications

Padraig Flynn:
Social Affairs and Employment; Relations with the Economic and Social Committee; Questions on Immigration and Home Affairs and Justice

Antonio Ruberti:
Science, Research and Development; Joint Research Centre; Human Resources, Education, Training and Youth

René Steichen:
Agriculture and Rural Development

Ioannis Paleokrassas:
Environment, Nuclear Safety and Civil Protection; Fisheries Policy

Raniero Vanni d'Archirafi:
Institutional Questions; Internal Market; Financial Services; Enterprise Policy – Small and Medium-sized Enterprises, Distributive Trades and Craft Sector

There are separate units, among others, for Consumer Protection and Human Resources, Education, Training and Youth.

In addition to the directorates-general, commissioners also have their own personal cabinets. These combine the functions which in Whitehall are carried out by the private office and the political advisers. The staff of a cabinet share their commissioner's term of office. Some of them are Commission officials on secondment from a directorate-general, to which they will return in due course. Others, like many of the commissioners themselves, expect to return to a role in national politics.

The Directors General are

DG	Director-General	Responsibilities
DG I	Horst G. Krenzler	External Relations
	Juan Prat	Mediterranean Policy, Relations with Latin America, North-South Relations (includes work on combating drug abuse in developing countries)
DG II	Giovanni Ravasio	Economic and Financial Affairs
DG III	Ricardo Perissich	Internal Market and Industrial Affairs
DG IV	Claus Dieter Ehlermann	Competition
DG V	Hywel Jones (acting)	Employment, Industrial Relations and Social Affairs (includes European Social Fund, Health and Safety at Work, AIDS, Cancer, Drug abuse)
DG VI	Guy Legras	Agriculture (includes rural development; also free food for distribution to needy people)
DG VII	Robert Coleman	Transport
DG VIII	To be appointed	Development (in developing countries)
DG IX	Frans de Koster	Personnel and Administration

DG X	Colette Flesch	Audiovisual Media, Information, Communication and Culture (includes Citizens' Europe)
DG XI	Laurens jan Brinkhorst	Environment, Nuclear Safety and Civil Protection
DG XII	Paolo Fasella	Science, Research and Development (includes biotechnology)
DG XIII	Michel Carpentier	Telecommunications, Information Technology and Innovation
DG XIV	Jose Almeida Serra	Fisheries
DG XV	Geoffrey Fitchew	Financial Institutions and Company Law
DG XVI	Eneko Landaburu Illarramendi	Regional Policies
DG XVII	Constaninos S. Maniatopulos	Energy
DG XVIII	Enrico Cioffi	Credit and Investments
DG XIX	Jean-Paul Mingasson	Budgets
DG XX	Lucien de Moor	Financial Control
DG XXI	Peter Willmot	Customs Union and Indirect Taxation
DG XXIII	Heinrich von Moltke	Enterprise Policy, Commerce, Tourism and Social Economy (includes co-operatives, and some work with non-governmental organisations)

1.2.2 Parliament

The European Parliament is currently composed of 518 elected representatives of the people of the European Community, although this number will increase to 567 in the 1994 elections, to take into account the unification of Germany. The Parliament's role is largely to advise on draft legislation, though under the Single European Act it has gained some new powers of amendment. The Single European Act introduced a new procedure. As before, legislation concerned with introducing the internal market goes from the Commission to the Parliament which gives an opinion. It then goes to the Council which, instead of making a final decision, adopts a 'common position' by qualified majority (see ss 1.2.4). The Parliament considers the common position and can either reject it (whereupon the Council can adopt it only by a unanimous vote), or amend it (whereupon it goes back to the Commission to produce a new version which the Council can adopt by qualified majority or amend by unanimity). If the Council does not act, the proposal lapses. These new powers for the Parliament have already been used to force member states to adopt strict new minimum standards for small car exhaust emissions. The Maastricht treaty increases Parliament's powers further for some areas of the EC's work. Under 'co-decision making', if the Council does not accept the Parliament's amendments a conciliation committee representing both sides is convened and the final say is with the Parliament. If, after this, it is still dissatisfied, Parliament can only reject a proposal by absolute majority.

As MEPs are elected by EC citizens, only those policies determined by co-decision have been made by people who are directly accountable to the electorate. All other decisions are indirectly accountable because they are made by ministers who answer only to their national parliament, or by the Commission.

Accountable and new activities include completion of outstanding single market measures, defining the right to live and work across EC, making degrees etc. mutually valid, trans-Europe transport, energy and tele-communications links, research and development, environmental action programmes, definition of EC-wide education co-operation and cultural action, public health and consumer laws, the new Cohesion Fund for poor regions, policies on industry and tourism.

Parliament shares with the Council the decisions on the Community's budget (see ss 1.2.5). The Parliament has, in effect, a veto on the accession of new states to the Community and on trade agreements with non-EC countries. The Maastricht Treaty extends this to international agreements which set up institutions or have significant financial implications, the uniform electoral system, citizenship, especially residence rights, the structural funds and the role of the European Central Bank. In theory it also has the power to dismiss the Commission (but not individual com-missioners). This power has never been exercised, though attempts have been made. The Maastricht Treaty gives Parliament the right to be consulted on the appointment of the President of the Commission.

Parliament is to appoint an ombudsman or woman to whom any citizen can complain about maladministration by any EC administration. The right to petition Parliament on matters within the EC's competence is also confirmed by the Maastricht treaty. The European Parliament will meet the national Parliaments from time to time in a Conference of Parliaments. It is to be consulted on the main features of European Union.

The Parliament's main location is Strasbourg. The Secretariat is based in Luxembourg. The plenary sessions are normally held in Strasbourg. Committee meetings are held in Brussels. This situation is forced on the Parliament by the obligation to share around the location of prestigious EC institutions between member states.

Groups

Members of the Parliament (MEPs) sit in transnational groups. Thus Labour MEPs from the United Kingdom sit in the Socialist Group and British Conservatives sit with the Group of the European People's Party. Until the next elections in June 1994, the Parliament will be comprised of (more or less) Socialists, 180; European People's Party, 162; Liberal, Democratic and Reformist, 45; European Democrats, 21; Greens, 27; plus four other groups and 12 non-attached MEPs.

Committees

Much of the work of the Parliament is done in committees. When proposed legislation reaches Parliament it is immediately referred to the appropriate committee which appoints a rapporteur and produces a draft opinion for consideration at a plenary session.

Some of the key Committees are

Committee and chair   *UK Members*

Committee and chair	UK Members
Agriculture, Fisheries and Rural Development Franco Borgho (Italy, PPE)	Henry McCubbin (Labour) David Morris (Labour) Revd Ian Paisley (DUP) Lord Plumb (Conservative) Richard Simmonds (Conservative) George Stevenson (Labour) Michael Welsh (Conservative) Joe Wilson (Labour)
Legal Affairs and Citizens' Rights Franz Ludwig Stauffenberg (Germany, Christian Democrat)	Geoffrey Hoon (Labour) Lord Inglewood (Conservative) Christine Oddy (Labour) Anthony Simpson (Conservative)
Social Affairs, Employment and the Working Environment Willem van Velzen (Netherlands, Socialist)	Hugh McMahon (Labour) Tom Megahy (Labour) Stephen Hughes (Labour) Lord O'Hagan (Conservative) John Stevens (Conservative) Carole Tongue (Labour)
Regional Policy and Regional Planning Antoni Gutierrez Diaz (Spain, GUE)	Wayne David (Labour) Alex Falconer (Labour) Paul Howell (Conservative) John Hume (SDLP) James Nicholson (OUP) Sir Christopher Prout (Conservative)

Environment, Public Health and Consumer Protection

Ken Collins
(UK, Socialist)

David Bowe (Labour)
Pauline Green (Labour)
Caroline Jackson (Conservative)
Anita Pollack (Labour)
Sir James Scott-Hopkins
(Conservative)
Tom Spencer (Conservative)
Ian White (Labour)

Youth, Culture, Education and the Media

Antonio la Pergola
(Italy, Socialist)

Michael Elliot (Labour)
Patricia Rawlings (Conservative)
Sir Jack Stewart-Clark
(Conservative)

Development and Co-operation

Henri Saby
(France, Socialist)

John Bird (Labour
Janey Buchan (Labour)
Margaret Daly (Conservative)
Winnie Ewing (SNP)
Edward Kellet-Bowman
(Conservative)
Alf Lomas (Labour)
Michael McGowan (Labour)
William Newton-Dunn
(Conservative)

Women's Rights

Christine Crawley
(Socialist, UK)

Lord O'Hagan (Conservative)
Anita Pollack (Labour)
Carole Tongue (Labour

Inter-groups

The structures and procedures of the Parliament have evolved with the different parliamentarians who have served in it. These are not modelled on any one national assembly but draw on many European traditions. One example is the inter-group. This is a group which draws MEPs from, at least potentially, all countries and all political persuasions. It owes much of its shape to the Westminster All Party Parliamentary Group. Inter-groups of particular interest to voluntary organisations include those on consumer affairs (chaired by Pauline Green, see ss 13.3.1); the family (chaired by Pierre Lataillade, Mairie d'Arcachon, Place Lucien de Gracia, 33120 Arcachon, France, Tel: 010 33 56 83 17 20); ageing (serviced by Eurolink Age see ss 4.3.2; disabled people (chaired by Derek Prag, see ss 7.3) and the social economy (chaired by Marie-Claude Vayssade of France).

1.2.3 Economic and Social Committee

The Economic and Social Committee gives opinions on certain proposals for legislation or action programmes. Its members, who are nominated by national governments, belong to one of three groups: Employers, Workers or 'Various Interests'. The Various Interests group has in the past been composed of experts, each drawn from a particular field such as farming, consumer affairs, local government, academia and professional groups. The UK membership of the committee for the four-year period which started in September 1990 is given in ss 2.6.1 (or in Vacher's *European Companion*, see ss 1.5.4). Just as the Parliament works mainly through committees, the Economic and Social Committee has sections which do the detailed work of preparing opinions.

The Economic and Social Committee has national analogues in France and Belgium and one or two other countries. Its discussions are less politicised than those of the Parliament and they are often better informed. They are, however, much less influential. The Committee is more aware of the work and concerns of non-governmental organisations than are other European Community institutions. It provides some of the European groupings with assistance with meeting rooms and interpretation – one of the main practical problems.

1.2.4 Council of Ministers

The Council of Ministers is the European Community institution which takes the final decision on the legislation and programmes proposed by the Commission. Participants in Council meetings change with the subjects under discussion. An Agriculture Council meeting brings together the ministers of agriculture, a Development Council, the ministers for overseas development, and so on. Meetings of the Council involve a relevant commissioner and the national ministers responsible for the subjects under consideration. Thus, the Minister for Agriculture, Fisheries and Food will normally attend an Agriculture Council meeting, and the Minister for Overseas Development a Development Council. United Kingdom ministers are supported by civil servants from their own departments and from the diplomatic mission to the Community. This mission is known as UKREP (the office of the UK Permanent Representative). It functions independently from the missions to NATO and Belgium which are also in Brussels.

The job of chairing Council meetings rotates among the governments of the member states. A country is in the chair for six months and is then replaced. At present the order is taken from an alphabetical list which depends upon the countries' own ways of spelling their names. The United Kingdom had the 'presidency' for the period July–December 1992. The country that holds the Presidency has a number of important tasks. As well as chairing meetings and trying to extract clear decisions from difficult discussions, it is responsible for the overall pattern of Council business during its six-month term. Its ambassadors around the world represent the member states' collective views on political questions to other countries (though on matters concerned with the working of the Community, eg external trade, the Commission represents the Community on the basis of a brief from the Council), Presidents are increasingly seeking continuity by collaborating in a 'Troika', involving the country that has just relinquished the presidency as well as the one which is preparing to take command.

Under the terms of the Single European Act, many of the decisions that are necessary for the completing of the internal market are taken by what is known as a 'qualified majority'. Under this system 76 votes are distributed among the countries so that larger countries receive more votes than smaller ones (though larger countries get fewer votes per inhabitant). Germany, France, Italy and the United Kingdom each have 10 votes, Spain 8, Belgium, Greece, the Netherlands and Portugal 5, Denmark and Ireland 3 and Luxembourg 2. For a qualified majority to be reached, 54 votes have to be in favour. Thus no two countries can block a vote. Maastricht extends qualified majority voting to some new areas, but the right of veto remains for most decisions on social policy, transport policy, citizenship, review of the research, regional and social funds, environment programmes and visa policy.

Before any proposal is put before a Council meeting it is prepared by a working group involving national civil servants, either from the diplomatic mission (UKREP in the case of the United Kingdom) or from the home department, and a Commission official. They report to a body called COREPER (the Committee of Permanent Representatives), which brings together the ambassadors of the member states. COREPER is responsible for deciding whether business is ready to go to Council either for confirmation of agreements already reached or for discussion of identified areas of disagreement.

Towards the end of each presidency the 'European Council' brings together the Heads of Government (and, in the case of France, the Head of State) with the president of the Commission. The Council has no role in the legislative process but provides political leadership and agrees on the broad outline of new developments. There is a tendency for the Council to be the climax of a government's efforts to achieve some progress in the European Community and it has been the occasion of some dramatic shifts in position.

1.2.5 The budget

The European Community financial year is the same as the calendar year. Each December a budget is agreed for the following year. Most of the work of the European Community is financed by what is known as 'own resources'. These include customs duties and agricultural levies, a proportion of VAT, and a new resource, which is based on GNP.

All European Community budgeting and accounting is done in ecus. The ecu is not yet a currency in day-to-day use. It is a notional unit, calculated by adding fixed amounts of the currencies in the European Monetary System. Its value is calculated on a daily basis on the exchange market rates and published in the press. In June 1993, the ecu was worth nearly 80p.

The process of deciding upon the budget is somewhat protracted, involving a proposal from the Commission and two readings each in the Parliament and the Council. The Parliament then has the power to reject the budget altogether, so that the process starts again with a new proposal from the Commission. Under the Maastricht Treaty, the Commission will no longer be able to withhold information from Parliament when it tables questions on the budget.

Usually the Council seeks to reduce spending (except on the CAP) and the Parliament to reinstate it. The Parliament and the Council each have areas of the budget on which theirs is the final word within the established total figure.

1.2.6 The Court of Justice

This has the power to impose fines on member states if they fail to implement EC laws, or comply with the Court's judgements.

1.3 Westminster and Whitehall

The important roles that politicians and civil servants from national administrations play in European Community decision making were demonstrated above. These people are excellent sources of information and are often very pleased to have access to the knowledge and views of voluntary organisations. They are also cheap to telephone.

Both Houses of Parliament have standing committees to monitor European Community developments. The House of Lords devotes considerable time to European Community matters. Its European

Communities Select Committee works through six specialised sub-committees. In the Commons a full debate is held before the European Council meetings, so that MPs have a greater chance of influencing the line taken by the Prime Minister at the meeting. In addition, informal links between the House of Commons and the European Parliament are to be encouraged.

1.4 Contacts

The Commission of the European Communities
Rue de la Loi 200
1049 Brussels
Belgium
Tel: 010 32 2 299 1111
(switchboard: English can be used)

The Commission has press and information offices in all European Community countries. In the United Kingdom the offices are:

8 Storey's Gate
London SW1P 3AT
Tel: 071-973 1992
Fax: 071-973 1900

Head of Office: Vacant (Geoffrey Martin, temporary)
Information: GianCarlo Pau

NB The London office has a comprehensive library which can be visited between 10am and 1pm daily and phoned between 2 and 5pm.

4 Cathedral Road	9 Alva Street	Windsor House
Cardiff CF1 9SG	Edinburgh EH2 3AT	9–15 Bedford Street
Tel: 0222-371631	Tel: 031-225 2058	Belfast BT2 7EG
Fax: 0222-395489	Fax: 031-226 4105	Tel: 0232-240708
Jorgen Hansen	Kenneth Munro	Fax: 0232-248241
		Jane Morris

European Parliament
Centre Européen	and at	and at
Plateau du Kirchberg	97–113 Rue Bélliard	Palais de l'Europe
PO Box 1601	1047 Brussels	BP 1024
Luxembourg	Belgium	F-67070 Strasbourg
Tel: 010 352 43001	Tel: 010 32 2 284 2111	France
	Fax: 010 32 2 230 6856	Tel: 010 33 88 17 40 01

15

The Parliament has an information office in London, which is closed to the public on Fridays. The staff can supply information about MEPs and about the progress of legislation through the Parliament. It is at

2 Queen Anne's Gate
London SW1H 9AA
Tel: 071-222 0411
Fax: 071-222 2713
Head: Martyn Bond

Economic and Social Committee
Rue Ravenstein 2
1000 Brussels
Belgium
Tel: 010 32 2 519 9011
Fax: 010 32 2 513 4893

Council of Ministers
Rue de la Loi 170
1048 Brussels
Belgium
Tel: 010 32 2 234 6111
Fax: 010 32 2 234 7397

UK Representation to the European Communities
6 Rond-Point Schuman
1040 Brussels
Belgium
Tel: 010 32 2 287 8211
Fax: 010 32 2 230 8379

A directory of UKREP officials appears in Vacher's *European Companion* (see ss 1.5.4).

Westminster
Dr C R M Ward
Clerk to the Committee
Select Committee on European
Legislation
House of Commons
London SW1A 0AA
Tel: 071-219 5467

P D G Hayter
Clerk of Committees Office
House of Lords
London SW1A 0PW
Tel: 071-219 3218

Sub-committees
A (Finance, Trade and Industry
and External Relations)
Mr Sneath
Tel: 071-219 5662

B (Energy, Transport and
Technology)
Mr Burton
Tel: 071-219 3150

C (Social and Consumer Affairs)

Dr Tudor
Tel: 071-219 3140

D (Agriculture and Food – covers
rural development)
Mr Ollard
Tel: 071-219 6083

E (Law and Institutions)
Mr Burton
Tel: 071-219 3150

F (Environment)
Mrs Martin
Tel: 071-219 3015

1.5 Progress towards European unity

1.5.1 The Single European Act and freedom of movement

The treaty amendment was agreed in 1987 under the title Single European Act. It restated the aims of the Community, added the target of completion of the Single Market by 1993, laid down the necessary components of a completed internal market and streamlined decision making, increasing the powers of the European Parliament and reducing the ability of one member state to block legislation. It also reaffirmed the Community's concern for economic and social cohesion and support for the poorer regions, formally added the environment to the Community's mandate (see chapter 11) established greater political co-operation among the 12 member states and made new arrangements to expedite the work of the European Court of Justice. The Single European Act's main aim is a single market without internal frontiers in which the free movement of goods, persons, services and capital is ensured.

The Single European Act has caused a dramatic change in the ability of the European Community to make decisions. The nature of the legislation that is being proposed has changed. Instead of trying to get everyone to agree on a harmonised specification of, say, a product, the assumption is now that anything which can legally be sold in one country of the Community can be legally sold in all the others. Now legislation only has to sort out any anomalies this creates and sometimes estabish common minimum standards for safety purposes. The decision making process has been improved.

1.5.2 Maastricht

The Maastricht Treaty, which was designed to help economic and political stability and deal with tensions of an expanding Community, was finally agreed on 11 December 1991, subject to ratification. It

- increases the accountability of the EC;
- defines subsidiarity, ie that EC laws should only be enacted if they can be more effective than regional or national laws;
- builds on the 1992 single market programme; and
- allows for enlargement by the addition of new members.

The Treaty's 250 pages amend 1,100 pages of existing EC treaties including the 1987 *Single European Act* and create a three-pillared arrangement called 'The European Union'. Of this the European Community is the central pillar. The two outer pillars cover areas of existing informal co-operation between governments, outside the structure of the EC: common foreign and security policy and home affairs and justice policy. The implications for the different sectors are dealt with in the relevant chapters but the EC's wider competence in consumer, health and education may lead to more funding programmes in those areas. The UK has chosen not to participate in the protocol which covers the Social Chapter and reserves the right not to proceed with monetary union, but it is involved in all discussions.

1.5.3 Economic union

At Maastricht member states agreed to adopt a common single currency from 1999, provided that they meet common targets on the stability of their exchange rates, the level of inflation and the size of any budget deficit. Their economies also have to have converged to a considerable extent. The UK is permitted to opt out of the process if it wishes to do so before a single currency (the ecu) and a Central Bank are introduced. In practice the changes involved in moving towards economic and monetary union cause problems for many countries. Even the Exchange Rate Mechanism (ERM) designed to stabilise exchange rates is under great strain. The UK left the ERM in 1992, specifying very restrictive conditions for returning to it.

1.5.4 Publications

1992 Eurospeak Explained, by Stephen Crampton, Rosters, 1990

The ABC of Community Law, European Documentation series, August 1990, available from the London office of the Commission, 8 Storey's Gate, London SW1P 3AT, Tel: 071-973 1992; Fax: 071-973 1900

Brussels in Focus, EC Access for Sport, by Bill Seary, Sports Council, December 1992, £10

A Citizen's Europe, European Documentation series, June 1991, available from the London office of the Commission, 8 Storey's Gate, London, SE1P 3AT, Tel: 071-973 1992; Fax: 071-973 1900

'EC Policymaking: Institutional Considerations', in *The European Community and the Challenge of the Future*, ed. by J. Lodge, Pinter Publishers, 1989

Economic and Monetary Union, European File series, May 1991, available from the London office of the Commission, 8 Storey's Gate, London SW1P 3AT, Tel: 071-973 1992; Fax: 071-973 1900

The Europe 1992 Directory, by A. Inglis and C. Hoskyns, ITCU/Coventry Polytechnic, available from ITCU, 189–191 Freston Road, London W10 6TH

Europe 2000: the development of the Community's territory, European File series, 1992, available from the London office of the Commission, 8 Storey's Gate, London SW1P 3AT, Tel: 071-973 1992; Fax: 071-973 1900

Europe in Ten Lessons, European Documentation series, May 1992, available from the London office of the Commission, 8 Storey's Gate, London SW1P 3AT, Tel: 071-973 1992; Fax: 071-973 1900

Europe, our Future – The Institutions of the European Community, 1991, available from the London Office of the Commission, 8 Storey's Gate, London SW1P 3AT, Tel: 071-973 1992; Fax: 071-973 1900

European constituencies and MEPs in the UK, a leaflet giving the names and constituencies of all UK MEPs available from the London Information Office of the European Parliament, 2 Queen Anne's Gate, London SW1H 9AA, Tel: 071-222 0411; Fax: 071-222 2713

The European Economic Arena, European File series, November 1991, available from the London office of the Commission, 8 Storey's Gate, London SW1P 8AT, Tel: 071-973 1992; Fax: 071-973 1900

European Union, European Documentation series, May, 1992, available free from the London office of the Commission, 8 Storey's Gate, London SW1P 3AT, Tel: 071-973 1992; Fax: 071-973 1900

Guide to the European Community – the Original and Definitive Guide to all aspects of the EC, published by The Economist Books Ltd., £20, available from The Economist Bookshop, 23a Ryder Street, London, SW1, Tel: 071-839 9104

PMS Parliamentary Companion, quarterly, includes some EC contacts, single copies £7.25, annual subscription £22, available from 19 Douglas Street, London SW1P 4PA

The Right to Petition the European Parliament, available from the London Information Office of the European Parliament, 2 Queen Anne's Gate, London SW1H 9AA, Tel: 071-222 0411; Fax: 071-222 2713

The Single Market in Action, European Documentation series, August 1992, available from the London office of the Commission, 8 Storey's Gate, London SW1P 3AT, Tel: 071-973 1992; Fax: 071-973 1900

Vacher's European Companion, the book with all the names you could want, available from Vacher's Publications, 113 High Street, Berkhamsted, Herts HP4 2DJ, Tel: 0442-876135

Working for Change in the European Community: a Guide to Successful Lobbying of the EC, available from WDM, 25 Beehive Place, London, SW9 7QR, Tel: 071-737 6215

Working Together – The Institutions of the European Community, 1991, available from the London office of the Commission, 8 Storey's Gate, London SW1P 3AT, Tel: 071-973 1992; Fax: 071-973 1900

2 Raising Money and Influencing Policy

This chapter will enable you to put the information in the rest of the book to good use. The suggestions made here will help any voluntary organisation, trade union or local authority which is planning an approach to the European Community.

2.1 Raising money from the European Community

2.1.1 Grants

Some people have been lucky but, by and large, obtaining European Community money is not easy. Although quite large sums of money are sometimes available, very little is specifically designated to voluntary organisations (with the exception of overseas development). Applying for European Community money is usually a long-winded process with, sometimes, a lot of paperwork involved.

The European Community normally makes grants for a limited period only, usually one year at a time. Once a grant has been awarded, the conditions are rarely amended – for example, to take account of inflation. The Commission requires careful bookkeeping. The allocations made are often slow in arriving. The rewards, however, can be high. Some voluntary organisations have received as much as £1 million in one year for a project. So it is certainly worth investigating your eligibility. This book shows you how to do so without committing a disproportionate amount of time to the task.

Use this book to see if your work coincides with areas of current European Community funding, or with subjects of interest to the European Community, which could be areas of future funding. You may need to do a bit of rethinking to bring your project within the Community's scope. For example, your general housing work may help a high proportion of immigrants. Perhaps that part of the project can be made eligible for funding as a scheme for immigrants. Is there scope for working with counterparts in the rest of the European Community or for making your project particularly relevant to a European Community policy area? A European slant will give you a much better chance of getting money.

It may be necessary to change your terminology. Can your work with the unemployed be regarded as vocational training? If renamed, it may attract money from the European Social Fund. For example, although the European Social Fund makes no provision for assistance for literacy programmes, operations of this type have in the past nevertheless received assistance when integrated into vocational programmes. Therefore, even if your project does not seem to fit, do some more checking.

The EC is increasingly using programmes, run by outside organisations or consultancies, to dispense funds. We have tried to include all the funds of most interest to voluntary organisations in the following chapters, but these programmes normally have a time limit of three years, although they may be renewed. The picture therefore changes rapidly and you may find that a new fund may have been established or the officials concerned may have enough flexibility to incorporate your scheme. Speak to one of the national contacts listed in the relevant chapter or to one of the contacts listed in ss 2.4.1.

Once you think you have a reasonable case to put or you have drawn a blank but want to be quite sure, contact the relevant officials. In the case of the European Social Fund and the European Regional Development Fund, you should write to the people in the United Kingdom mentioned in ss 3.3.1. In other cases, write direct to the contact at the Commission in Brussels.

Explain what you want to do on no more than two and a half sides of paper. As well as sending you an application form, if needed, the official will be able to indicate when a decision can be expected and what the normal size for a grant is. It is important not to ask for much more than this or your application may not be considered. If you do not get a reply within three weeks, telephone the official for an answer.

When to apply

Applications normally stand the best chance of being accepted if submitted late in one year for funding in the next. The European Community financial year runs from January to December so officials often decide how to allocate most of their money in January. Sometimes pockets of money become available at odd times, however. Another project may fall through or an extra allocation may be made. Occasionally an unexpected surplus needs to be spent quickly at the end of the year. Even if you have missed a deadline, it is worth making an approach for information about future availability of funding. The European Social Fund has its own rules for the timing of applications (see ss 3.4.1).

In some cases you will need the financial backing of United Kingdom national or local government and, in all cases, its moral support for your work can only help. It is particularly important to get this if European Community support is going to be only for a short time. You may need government funding to keep your project going afterwards. Also mention to the Commission any famous patrons. Some of the specialised programmes have advisory committees which can serve as a useful information route into the Commission for voluntary organisations.

2.1.2 Studies and research contracts

The alternative to asking the Commission for money is to offer to carry out some particular activity for them. This is quite a common practice as the Commission does not have the resources to do all the tasks that arise, particularly in response to pressure from the European Parliament. Unfortunately, there is no easy way to discover what contracts are on offer at any particular time. Most tenders are printed in the *Official Journal* and you can scan that, or, more easily, pay a commercial concern to do it for you. Many of the users of this book, however, will be interested in smaller contracts. These are normally put out to tender among the organisations that the Commission knows might be interested. Success in this field undoubtedly goes mainly to the organisations that make a point of cultivating contacts with Commission officials.

Some organisations have successfully stood the process on its head. They have persuaded the Commission, often with help from the European Parliament, that their particular area of expertise is one that the European Community needs to be better informed about. More often than not they will be the people asked to carry out the work.

2.2 Exerting influence

The European Community affects us all directly or indirectly and it is natural that we should try to have some influence over the decisions that it takes. This influence can often be achieved indirectly: Westminster MPs, Ministers and United Kingdom civil servants are all in the business of defending our interests. There are times, however, when a voluntary organisation needs to raise an issue which is specific to it and which our representatives may not understand or may not feel is of sufficiently general United Kingdom interest. That organisation will have to make its voice heard at European Community level.

In theory the policy formation process is simple. Proposals are framed by the Commission. They are commented on by the European Parliament and the Economic and Social Committee. Finally the Council makes the decision which then becomes part of European legislation or agreed policy. Anyone with a particular concern needs to ensure that it is raised in an appropriate way by the Commission. They then need to ensure that European Parliament and Economic and Social Committee comments are helpful. Finally they need to bring influence to bear on the ministers who are going to sit round the Council table. On this simple model the steps one needs to take are clear if not particularly easy.

2.2.1 Lobbying the Commission

The Commission is the only European Community body which can formally initiate a proposal. This makes it the first target of all lobbyists. What proposals it makes and what the contents of those proposals are have enormous influence over the Community policy formation process. In the past the Commission has been a remarkably open bureaucracy. It is less so now as its importance increases and as its staff get busier and busier. It is still, however, noticeably easier to engage in policy discussions with Commission officials than it is with civil servants in Whitehall, especially if you can claim to represent a trans-European organisation.

Although it is open to the outside world, the Commission is not particularly good on internal communication, so it is up to you to identify the best division to contact. Later chapters in this book will get you started in the right direction. The best way of getting in touch is by writing a letter or sending a fax. Make it short and to the point. There is a good chance that the recipient will not have English for their mother tongue. Similarly many officials have never lived in the United Kingdom so it is important not to assume too much knowledge of the cultural background to your work. Do not be afraid to write in English, though, as most officials can read it and those who cannot have access to people who can interpret it for them.

Do not expect an early response to your letter. The post to Brussels works fairly well, but once inside the Commission letters can get passed from desk to desk. Incidentally, while they are often passed down the hierarchy, the reverse flow is unusual, so letters should be addressed to a fairly senior official. The problem is increased by language difficulties and bureaucratic procedures about who is allowed to sign what. Requests for application forms or documents that can be sent out with a compliments slip are not affected, but anything involving a statement of policy of any kind runs the risk of delay.

After two or three weeks you may have received a reply. If you have not, you need to approach the official concerned. This is best done by telephone, which may seem expensive (around 40p for each minute at the time of writing) but does have the advantage of giving you a real feel for the official's thinking. If yours is a small, under-funded organisation, it is possible to ask the official concerned to phone you back. Commission officials are likely to be at their desks from before 9am (8am in the United Kingdom for much of the year) to after 5.30pm (4.30pm in the UK). Long lunches are still the rule, though, so phone calls between 12.30 and 3pm, (11.30am–2pm) may not get much response. Each official has his or her own telephone number which can be dialled direct. Wherever possible these have been given in this book. Otherwise the Commission switchboard (010 32 2 299 1111) will connect you. The operators can all speak English. If you have difficulty gaining access to the Commission, your MEP might like to help you. If he or she writes on your behalf, you will get your reply or your meeting much more quickly. MEPs are generally quite keen to help voluntary organisations in their own constituencies.

Once you are in contact with an official you can ask whether your area of interest is under discussion and, if so, what initial thoughts the Commission has. It is not at all uncommon for voluntary organisations to find that their views are shared by the Commission and then officials can become very useful allies. They are always interested in ideas which might form the basis of a new initiative, but you have to remember that their interests are European ones. They are likely to be especially pleased to see groups with good links in several, if not all, Community countries. They will not be very helpful if they think your concerns are purely national ones and they are restricted by what in the jargon is called 'the principle of subsidiarity'. In the European Community context this means that the Community acts when the set objectives can be reached more effectively at its level than at that of the member states. In practice, and taking in particular the field of social affairs, the principle of subsidiarity means that the Commission will often limit its proposals to exchanges of one kind and another, leaving national or regional government to set standards and enforce legislation. Keep any meeting with officials as brief as you can; don't quote them without permission; and ask, if you may, before taking notes.

You may feel that your views and experience will make an important contribution to Commission thinking. In this case you will want to consider the possibility of asking for a meeting with the relevant Commissioner. While you are in Brussels you could also have separate meetings with officials and perhaps press your views on the UK Commissioners or their cabinets. The Commission as a whole takes responsibility for its decisions so all Commissioners have some influence over all decisions as well as having particular responsibility for their own portfolio. Someone within each cabinet will have responsibility for your subject and, although their responsibility is to act in the Community interest rather than a national one, it is likely that UK officials will understand what you are trying to achieve better than others. Virtually all Commissioners, and some of their cabinet staff, come from a background of national politics and probably intend to return to it, which encourages them to keep in touch with the specific concerns of their country.

2.2.2 Lobbying the Parliament and the Economic and Social Committee

So now the Commission has issued a proposal. This will normally take the form of a 'COM' document. That is an official communication from the Commission. It will have a number which in 1994, for example, has the form 'COM(94) xxx final', where xxx is a serial number. Getting a copy of this document quickly can be difficult. The best bet is normally the Commission official with whom you have already made friends or the relevant UK government department. The normal channels for buying documents can take a little while to get stocks.

The Parliament is likely to start work on forming an opinion very soon after the proposal has been adopted by the Commission. For many proposals, the Parliament's role is more significant now and the majority of the Parliament's changes to draft legislation are accepted by the Council and incorporated into final legislation.

One of the ways of raising an issue with the Parliament is to send it a 'petition'. Any European Community citizen can address a request or complaint to the European Parliament provided that they give their name, occupation, nationality and permanent address. Petitions go to a committee which examines them, decides upon their admissibility and takes any action it thinks appropriate. This can take the form of a report to the plenary session of the Parliament.

In Great Britain we have an easy route to the Parliament. Unlike the other MEPs, those from Great Britain are elected on a constituency basis. Your local MEP is always worth contacting when you are taking some new initiative. The United Kingdom MEPs on the Parliament's relevant committee (see ss 1.2.2) are also an excellent route for making a contribution to the discussion of proposals. It is not necessary to have a European Community-wide concern to contact an MEP, but he or she will have a much greater influence on Committee discussion if colleagues from other countries are sympathetic. The MEPs themselves can help with this (notably through the other main focus of their lives – the political group), but it will certainly be an advantage if you have contacts elsewhere. International groupings of non-governmental organisations have made very effective use of the plenary sessions in Strasbourg for lobbying. It is sometimes possible, for instance, to mount an exhibition inside the Palais de l'Europe. This catches MEPs when they have a slightly freer moment. Meetings are not so useful as normally very few MEPs can arrange to attend, though some non-governmental organisations do find inter-group meetings (see ss 1.2.2) are worth cultivating.

Contacting MEPs in person can be a chancy business. They tend to be in Strasbourg (for a plenary session) and Brussels (for a committee meeting) at least once each month. In addition, they normally have a political group meeting to go to in Brussels. They also need to spend some time in their constituency, which for the lucky ones is also their home. All MEPs have assistants either in their constituency or in Brussels or both. These people travel less. They are often very well informed and helpful, so they provide a useful first port of call in any lobbying exercise.

In general terms, approaching the Economic and Social Committee is very much the same. Members of the committee do not have to face frequent trips to Luxembourg or Strasbourg but they are in Brussels often, several times each month in most cases. They do not have geographical constituencies, but they do concentrate their efforts in particular subject sections, rather similar to parliamentary committees. Their equivalent of a political group is the way they are divided among workers, employers and various interests. The Trades Union Congress (TUC) and the Confederation of British Industry (CBI) are the best contact points for the first two groups. The others, who can be very sympathetic to voluntary organisations, need to be contacted directly (see ss 1.2.3 for more information on the Economic and Social Committee).

2.2.3 Lobbying the Council

The Council is the most powerful of the Community institutions. It normally has the final word on legislation and policy matters. It is more difficult to reach than the other institutions. By the time that proposals get to ministers, or even to the Committee of Permanent Representatives (COREPER), there is little scope for changing national positions. In this institution, national interests are paramount. The point of the Council is that by giving national governments the final say on most legislation, it ensures that they are by and large willing to implement it.

The main arenas for lobbying the Council are therefore in national capitals. You need to find out which civil servant is responsible for the negotiations in the Council working group. He or she will be responsible for interpreting United Kingdom policy at group meetings. It may well be, though, that you believe that policy should change and then Ministers and your own MP should be approached. It is often useful to keep members of the House of Lords informed, especially those who serve on the European Communities Select Committee (see s 1.4.1).

The main way of lobbying other governments is through non-governmental organisations in their country. See s 2.4 below for some hints on how to start to make contact.

2.3 Putting it all together

The preceding sections have assumed a simple model of European Community policy formation in which the Commission proposes, the Parliament comments and the Council decides. In real life things are more complicated. All the institutions spend some of their time trying to influence the others. The Commission is always represented at Parliamentary plenary sessions and frequently takes the floor. Commission officials sit with Council working groups. Council meetings involve a Commissioner. The Parliament frequently passes resolutions calling on the Commission to make proposals on particular subjects. It uses its powers over the budget to shape Commission spending and hence the areas in which it is active. The Council is also represented at plenary sessions of the Parliament. It, too, passes resolutions calling for Commission proposals. In addition to these formal links between the institutions there is a constant informal to-ing and fro-ing which also involves the national civil servants.

In practice this means that lobbying needs to proceed on all fronts at once. The priority at any one time will depend upon who has shown interest as well as upon the stage that has been reached in the legislative process. Any press coverage you can get along the way can only be helpful.

2.4 Networking

For more detailed information on working with a European network, see the NCVO book, *Networking in Europe*. However, the following section will give you some guidance on existing networks, how to set up a new network and the legal framework.

2.4.1 Key contacts

For the networks that exist at the European Community level in your field, see the relevant chapter. Nigel Tarling at NCVO (address below) may be able to put you in contact with yet others.

Generalist networks

European Council of Voluntary Organisations (CEDAG)
18, Rue de Varenne
75007 Paris
France
Tel: 010 33 1 45 49 06 58
Fax: 010 33 1 42 84 04 84
Contact: Anne David

UK member:
NCVO,
Regents Wharf, 8 All Saints Street, London N1 9RL, Tel: 071-713 6161;
Fax: 071-713 6300
This organisation brings together organisations with a general interest in
the non-governmental sector. It is concentrating its initial efforts on the
consultative and legal status of European Community-wide organisations.

Euro Citizen Action Service (ECAS)
Rue Defacqz, 1, Boite 20
1050 Brussels
Belgium
Tel: 010 32 2 534 5166
Fax: 010 32 2 534 5275
Contact: Tony Venables
A non-profit organisation, working for other non-profit organisations.
The services it provides include information provision, advice on lobbying
and the use of an office in Brussels.

European Foundation Centre
Rue de la Concorde 51
1050 Brussels
Belgium
Tel: 010 32 2 512 8938
Fax: 010 32 2 512 3265
Contact: John Richardson
An information resource and meeting point for grant-making trusts. The
European Foundation Centre is intending to publish a directory of such
bodies.

Observatories

A useful source of contacts is also the observatories, set up by the
Commission to observe and report on social or regional events. There are
now observatories on cross-border co-operation, homelessness, the family,
employment and poverty.

2.4.2 Setting up a new network

You may discover that none of the existing networks exactly meets your
needs: your subject may be very specialised, you may be concerned about a
particular European Community proposal, or you may need a sympathetic
network in order to apply for a grant from, for example, the HELIOS

programme (see ss 7.4.1). If what you need does not exist you have to go out and create it. This section gives you some hints on doing this. But first, a word of warning: the task is not an easy one. You will have to work with people who, even if they have the same objectives as you, have a different cultural and probably linguistic background. The scope for misunderstanding is enormous. Also enormous is the commitment of time and money that will be needed. Travel costs cannot really be ignored, and though continental travel is often better value than that within the UK, the total soon mounts. Any serious meeting is going to have to find a way of working in a minimum of two languages. A room equipped for simultaneous interpretation is not cheap, and the interpreters themselves are normally very expensive. All in all, you need to have a very good reason and the full support of your organisation before contemplating starting a new network.

However, it can be done; none of the problems is totally insoluble. First of all you need to identify the other possible members of your new organisation. You probably have some contacts already. You need to build on these by word of mouth, by studying any of the host of European Community bulletins which are related to your area, by talking to Commission officials and MEPs. You need a list that is strong, in the sense that it has on it people from most EC countries and organisations which command respect in their national settings. The list should not be too long, which would make the early stages unwieldy. Much of the preparation can be done by one or two people who are able to spend time on writing, phoning and occasional bits of travel. Before your new organisation can be launched there will need to be a meeting of founding members. One of the best ways of arranging this is to combine it with an expert seminar on your topic. You should ask the Commission to host this (providing the travel costs, room and the interpreters), or to make a grant towards your costs in organising it. You can also approach trusts who might be more interested in the report of a seminar than they would be in the formation of a new international organisation. For the launch meeting you will need to have developed clear but not inflexible proposals for the staffing, activities, funding and constitution of your network. In developing proposals you will want to study the established European Community non-governmental organisations. These often rely on the Commission. Their activities are related to Commission activities and their funding (and therefore staffing) is supported to a greater or lesser extent by Commission grants or contracts for studies. Most of them also charge a membership fee which is sometimes on a scale which protects the poorest organisations or the organisations which face the greatest costs in participating in activities.

2.5 Community activities concerning non-governmental organisations

2.5.1 Legal and consultative status

In many European Community countries, associations are only strictly legal if they are registered with some level of government. This registration is often the key to some tax advantages and it may also give legal personality (so that an association can, for instance, own property or conduct law suits in its own name), but the historical root in at least some countries has more to do with a desire by governments to control possible nests of sedition than to recognise the value of the work done by voluntary organisations. Whatever the origins, non-governmental organisations elsewhere expect to have to register and are often ill at ease if this is not possible.

This raises particular problems for European Community-wide groupings because there is no registration procedure for them at Community level. In addition, national provisions are often not open to organisations the majority of whose committee members are not resident in the country concerned. Luckily, Belgium is an exception and many of the EC NGOs based there are registered as associations *sans but lucratif* or *'asbl's* (non-profit making associations) under Belgian law. This situation is, however, not satisfactory and the European Commission has produced a regulation which, if agreed by the Council of Ministers, would give formal, legal recognition to European voluntary organisations.

This may seem of fairly marginal interest, but it could be a useful step forward in another battle. For many years, non-governmental organisations have been urging the Commission to establish formal consultative procedures. Such procedures exist in both the United Nations family of organisations and in the Council of Europe. They have never been established in a general way for European Community institutions, though Directorate-General VIII (Overseas Development) has arrangements which approach them. Consultative status would mean that registered organisations would be entitled to have access to relevant documents and their views would need to be given due consideration.

2.5.2 Symbiosis and Citizens' Europe

Citizens' Europe aims to strengthen and promote the EC's identity and its image both for citizens and for the rest of the world. Some of the programme is of a public relations nature. A common design for passports is one example. Others are sponsorship of sports events and the like and increased use of the European flag and the European anthem.

Many are practical measures to enable individuals to benefit from freedom of movement. Citizens' Europe has led to information offices of the

Commission establishing advice services so that individuals can check on their rights in the Community. At the London Office of the European Commission the Citizens' Europe Advisory Service is available on Monday afternoons from 2pm to 5pm to advise individuals by telephone (071-973 1904) about their rights in the European Community.

Symbiosis is a programme of Directorate-General X (Information) of the Commission, part of the Citizens' Europe activity. It is an interactive European network linking European associations, local groupings and other networks involved in European integration, launched in 1990. For details contact Mrs Enrico Varese at the Commission, Rue de la Loi 200, 1049 Brussels, Tel: 010 32 2 299 4995.

2.5.3 The social economy

Directorate-General XXIII of the Commission has been given the task of dealing with this sector which covers co-operatives, mutual organisations (such as building societies) and non-governmental organisations. This includes the possibility of finding a legal structure for NGOs which cannot be regarded as having 'economic' activities. Those that do have such activities are thought to be covered by the established arrangements for European Economic Interest Groups.

2.6 Getting up-to-date information

2.6.1 Contacts

European Documentation Centres

These have complete sets of the publications of the Community. This material should be readily accessible and the centres are often staffed by people who can guide you through the intricacies. There are 44 European Documentation Centres in the United Kingdom, based mainly in universities and polytechnics. A list is available from the London office of the Commission, 8 Storey's Gate, London SW1P 3AT, Tel: 071-973 1992; Fax: 071-973 1900.

Information offices of the Commission and the Parliament (see s 1.4)

These are conveniently placed for visitors to central London. The staff of the Commission office are desperately overloaded with enquiries but the library can be consulted and it is a useful alternative to the Documentation Centres. The Parliament office supplies a good deal of information about MEPs and about the progress of proposals through the Parliament. It can arrange for you to get briefing documents and summary reports for each plenary.

The London office of the Parliament will also supply, free, a full list of MEPs with their addresses, committees, etc – even their dates of birth. Particularly relevant United Kingdom MEPs are listed in ss 1.2.2.

Both the Conservative and Labour Groups of MEPs have offices in the building of the London office of the Parliament, 2 Queen Anne's Gate, London SW1H 9AA, Tel: 071-222 1719 (Labour) or 071-222 1720 (Conservative).

Economic and Social Committee

The following is a list of members of the 'various interests section' of the Economic and Social Committee. For contact details write to the National Council for Voluntary Organisations (NCVO), Regents Wharf, 8 All Saints Street, London N1 9RL, Tel: 071-713 6161; Fax: 071-713 6300. NCVO can also give advice on the way in which voluntary organisations can work with the institutions of the European Community.

Robert Moreland	former MEP
Professor William Black	formerly at Queens University, Belfast
Wilfred Aspinal	Managerial, Professional and Staff Liaison Group
Michael Strauss	National Farmers' Union
Jocelyn Barrow	Broadcasting Standards Council
Angela Guillaume	European Union of Women

The CBI and TUC contacts for members of the committee are:

Clare Hollingsworth
European Community Affairs Group
Confederation of British Industry
Centre Point
103 New Oxford Street
London WC1A 1DU
Tel: 071-379 7400 ext 2632
Fax: 071-240 1578

Tom Jenkins
International Dept.
TUC
Congress House
Great Russell Street
London WC1B 3LS
Tel: 071-636 4030 ext 191
Fax: 071-636 0632

The CBI also have a Brussels office: contact Dick Eberlie, director, Tel: 010 32 2 231 0465.

Local Government International Bureau

This is a good source of information on any European Community matter that might affect local government. Address: 35 Great Smith Street, London SW1P 3BJ, Tel: 071-222 1636.

2.6.2 Publications

Changing Europe, Challenges facing the voluntary and community sectors in the 1990s, by Sean Baine, John Benington and Jill Russell, NCVO, 1992, £7.95

A Citizen's Europe, in the Europe on the move series, EC Commission, obtainable from the Commission's information offices, 8 Storey's Gate, London SW1P 3AT, Tel: 071-973 1992; Fax: 071-973 1900

'COM' documents can also be consulted at the European Documentation Centres. The official source in the United Kingdom is HMSO or its sub-agent Alan Armstrong Ltd, 2 Arkwright Road, Reading RG2 0SQ, Tel: 0734-751855; Fax: 0734-755164. See ss 2.2.2 for further advice about getting COM documents

EC Funding for Academic Research, by Michael Hopkins, European Research Centre, Loughborough University, Loughborough LE11 3TU

EC Research Funding available from the information offices of the Commission, 8 Storey's Gate, London SW1P 3AT, Tel: 071-973 1992; Fax: 071-973 1900

European Information Service, available from Local Government International Bureau, 35 Great Smith Street, London SW1P 3BJ, Tel: 071-222 1636

Networking in Europe, by Brian Harvey, NCVO, 1992

The *Official Journal* (OJ), available at European Documentation Centres and the London office of the Commission, is the key periodical. This includes all Commission proposals and Council decisions. A separate series gives a complete record of parliamentary proceedings

Social Europe, The Commission's review. It is available through HMSO and should be available for consultation at European Documentation Centres.

3 Unemployment

This chapter covers European Community funded schemes for creating jobs, training and helping unemployed people. It will be of interest to voluntary organisations, charities and churches working with unemployed people, co-operatives, trade unions, careers advisers, training centres, those involved in adult education, youth organisations, local authorities and businesses.

3.1 Key Commission departments

Commissioner: Padraig Flynn (Irish)
Task Force for Human Resources, Education, Training and Youth. Director: Thomas O'Dwyer, Tel: 010 32 2 295 8535; Fax: 010 32 2 295 7295

Employment, Industrial Relations and Social Affairs: Directorate-General V. Acting Director-General: Hywel Jones, Tel: 010 32 2 295 5722; Fax: 010 32 2 295 8690

European Social Fund (ESF): Otto Dibelius (German, speaks English), Tel: 010 32 2 295 4135

Key officials concerned with United Kingdom ESF applications: Levi Vermelho (Portuguese, speaks English)

Head of Division concerned with employment policies: John Morley (British), Tel: 010 32 2 295 1098

Commissioner: Bruce Millan (Scots)

Regional Policy: Directorate-General XVI

Director-General: Eneko Landaburu Illarramendi, Tel: 010 32 2 295 3046

Officials in charge of applications: from Great Britain – Graham Meadows, Tel: 010 32 2 295 6181; from Northern Ireland: Esben Poulsen, Tel: 010 32 2 295 0007/9578

3.2 Extent of Community involvement

The Treaty of Rome, which set up the European Economic Community, established a European Social Fund (ESF) (in articles 123–127) to promote employment opportunities and geographical and occupational mobility for workers within the Community. Article 128 also calls for the establishment of general principles for implementing a Community vocational training policy. The Community has a special interest in people made unemployed as an indirect result of its own policies in the agricultural, textile and steel sectors.

3.2.1 Social Chapter

In December 1989, 11 of the member states – ie all except for the United Kingdom – agreed to a Charter of the Fundamental Rights of Workers commonly known as the Social Chapter. The Social Chapter is an attempt to prevent employers from using the new opportunities of 1992 to the disadvantage of their employees. One specific worry is that employers will concentrate productive capacity in the countries with the lowest standards of social security, employment protection and trade union rights. The Social Chapter identifies the areas needing attention as freedom of movement, employment and remuneration, improvement of living and working conditions, social protection, freedom of association, vocational training, equal treatment for men and women, participation of workers, health and safety at work, child and youth labour, elderly people and disabled people. The Commission has now put forward detailed proposals for legislation on many of these.

3.2.2 The Structural Funds

Since 1975, when the European Regional Development Fund (ERDF) was established, extra European Community money has been allocated for employment in the less developed regions. The Single European Act (see s 1.4.1) called for a review of the ERDF, the ESF and the Agricultural Guidance Fund. This review was completed in 1988 and, as a result, the funds available to the three structural funds were doubled. They are subject to review again in 1993. The new framework of structural funds will run from 1994 to 1999, on a basis due to be agreed in summer 1993. The structural funds currently work collectively towards five objectives:

(i)   promoting the development and structural adjustment of the less developed regions;

(ii) converting the regions, frontier regions or parts of regions (including employment areas and urban communities) seriously affected by industrial decline;

(iii) combating long-term unemployment;
(iv) facilitating the occupational integration of young people; and
(v) reforming the Common Agricultural Policy, speeding up the adjustment of agricultural structures and promoting the development of rural areas.

In the United Kingdom the first objective applies to Northern Ireland. From 1994 it is expected that Merseyside and the Highlands and Islands of Scotland will also be included. The areas covered by the second and the last objectives are described in broad terms in the box below. Objective 5b is expected to be allocated between 6 and 7 billion ecu in the period 1993–9. A new Objective 4 is designed to help workers adapt to industrial change, to slow the increase in unemployment. A new Objective 3 has also been proposed, with more flexible criteria governing project eligibility. More detailed information is available from the sources listed in ss 3.3.1.

The Maastricht Treaty proposes to set up a Cohesion Fund by the end of 1993 which would provide financial aid to Ireland, Greece, Portugal and Spain. Northern Ireland is not included. Both trans-European communications networks, from which the UK will benefit, and environmental protection measures will be funded by this fund, which is in addition to the regional and social funds. The new framework of structural funds from 1994 to 1999 will have a total budget of 141.5 billion ecu. The Cohesion countries will have 15.5 billion ecu allocated, while 26.3 billion ecu is being set aside for the remaining Objective 1 countries.

European structural funds priority areas in the UK

Objective 1
Highlands and Islands of Scotland, Merseyside, Northern Ireland

Industrial Decline

Objective 2
Northumberland (Alnick, Amble, Morpeth, Ashinton, Newcastle-upon-Tyne), Tyne and Wear, Durham, Cleveland, Humberside (Doncaster, Goole, Selby, Grimsby, Hull, Scunthorpe), South Yorkshire, West Yorkshire (Bradford, Castleford, Pontefract, Wakefield, Dewsbury), Nottinghamshire (Gainsborough, Mansfield, Nottingham City UPA, Retford, Worksop), Greater Manchester, Lancashire (Accrington, Rossendale, Blackburn, Bolton, Bury, Burnley, Liverpool, Pendle, Rochdale, Wigan, St Helens), Merseyside, West Midlands, Fife (Alloa, Dunfermline, Dundee, Kirkcaldy), Central (Alloa, Falkirk, Glasgow, part of Stirling), Strathclyde (Ayr, Cumnock, Sanquhar, Dumbarton, Girvan, Glasgow, Greenock, Irvine, Kilmarnock, Lanarkshire), Gwent (Ebbw Vale, Abergavenny, Merthyr,

Rhymney, Newport, Pontypool, Cwmbran), Mid Glamorgan, West Glamorgan, Clwyd (Flint, Rhyl, Wrexham)
Assistance may be given to areas which are adjacent to these and to areas suffering from decline in vital industrial sectors.

Rural Development

Objective 5b
Highlands and Islands Development Board area, Isles of Scilly, part of Dumfries and Galloway, parts of Dyfed, Powys and Gwynedd, parts of Devon and Cornwall

The Treaty setting up the European Coal and Steel Community makes provision, in article 56, for financing programmes for the creation of new activities and for granting aid for the retraining and resettlement of workers in the coal and steel industries. The Community has a long-standing interest in local employment initiatives and has supported a number of activities in this area.

3.3 Key people

3.3.1 On fund applications

European Social Fund
Chris Evans, NCVO
Rita Narayan-Bhairo, Department of Employment, ESF Section, 236 Gray's Inn Road, London WC1X 8HL, Tel: 071-211 4732; Fax: 071-211 4749

European Regional Development Fund
Chris North, Department of Trade and Industry, Investment and Development Division, 232 Kingsgate House, 66–74 Victoria Street, London SW1E 6SW, Tel: 071-215 2556.

3.3.2 On policy issues

In the United Kingdom

Peter Haslett, Confederation of British Industry, Centre Point, 103 New Oxford Street, London WC1A 1DU, Tel: 071-379 7400, ext. 2618
David Lea, Trades Union Congress, 1 Congress House, Great Russell Street, London WC1B 3LS, Tel: 071-636 4030
Tom Megahy, MEP (Labour), 3 Burton Street, Wakefield, West Yorkshire WF1 2DD, Tel: 0924-382396

In Brussels

Peter Coldrick, European Trades Union Confederation (ETUC), Rue Montagne aux Herbes Potagères 37, 1000 Brussels, Tel: 010 32 2 209 2411
Renate Hornung-Draus, Union of the Industries of the European Communities (UNICE), Rue Joseph II 40, Boîte 4, 1040 Brussels, Tel: 010 32 2 237 6511; Fax: 010 32 2 231 1445
Dominique Geeroms, Youth Forum of the European Communities, 120 Rue Joseph II, 1040 Brussels, Tel: 010 32 2 230 6490

In the Netherlands and Brussels

D. Wijgaerts, European Centre for Work and Society
Netherlands address: Hoogbrugstraat 43, PO Box 3073, 6202 NB Maastricht, Tel: 010 31 43 216724; Fax: 010 31 43 255712
Belgian address: Tweeker Kenstraat 37, Brussels, Tel: 010 32 2 230 4339; Fax: 010 32 2 230 6404

The aim of the ECWS is to aid the overall development of work-related policies and to asssess their social and economic impact in a European context. Activities focus on four main areas: (i) employment policy; (ii) vocational training and technological change; (iii) specific groups in the labour market; and (iv) the organisation of work and new job profiles.

3.4 Funding

3.4.1 European Social Fund

Despite its name, the Social Fund deals with the labour market rather than with welfare questions. Its activities are largely concerned with vocational training programmes. Much of its assistance goes directly to governments to help fund their national programmes. In Great Britain about 50 per cent of the ESF funding assists government programmes for the unemployed. Many other sponsors are eligible for support, but the ESF will only match money (up to 45 per cent of costs) that has been promised by local or central government or other agreed public sources.

The ESF now has a budget of over 4 billion ecu benefiting about 2.8 million people per year. In 1991, £400 million was allocated to 12,500 British projects including government programmes, local projects organised by voluntary NGOs and the public sector, and training programmes organised in specific areas. The projects which are most likely to obtain funding are those providing regeneration in areas of severe industrial decline, work for long-term unemployed adults or under 25s, and those promoting the development of rural areas. There are only limited funds for career guidance and for training projects for groups such as women, ethnic minorities, migrants, refugees and people with disabilities although women and those 'socially excluded from the labour market' are recommended for a higher priority.

Past projects

Since the ESF was reformed at the end of 1989 many organisations have received grants ranging from a few thousand to over a million pounds for a year's project. In the voluntary sector, for example, projects have provided training, including how to set up co-operatives, and some job creation or work experience schemes. A number of charities have had sizeable grants for the vocational training of people with mental disabilities. Grants have been crucial to the development of women's training workshops. The Refugee Council has been able to run a major programme of combined vocational training and language training, and Community Service Volunteers received help for work experience for disadvantaged and unemployed young people.

Present arrangements

The Structural Funds are being reviewed in September 1993. At present, the ESF contributes to all five objectives set up in the last reform, but the majority of its activities concern Objective 3 (combating long-term unemployment) and Objective 4 (facilitating the occupational integration of young people). Commission guidelines for these objectives spell out ways in which the European Social Fund could contribute to reducing the inequalities in the Community's society and making it fairer. More emphasis is likely to be placed in future on promoting equal opportunities for men and women, including by the provision of childminding facilities. The adult 'long-term unemployed' are defined as those over 25 who have been unemployed for more than 12 months although the 12 month rule may be relaxed in future. 'Young people' are those between the age at which they have left full-time compulsory schooling and 25. A significant proportion of the European Social Fund is allocated to helping these two groups.

As far as the long-term unemployed are concerned, priority for funding is given to schemes which give this group training to vocational qualification or similar; are suited to the needs of the labour market; are linked with periods of work experience; and provide good value, in economic and social terms, for the money spent. Opportunities for recruitment to new but stable jobs, for the creation of self-employment activities, and for the employment of women after a long break in employment, are all important considerations.

To promote young people's integration into the labour market, the

Fund will pay particular attention to schemes for training, to a high level of qualification, young people who leave school without such qualifications; for training linked to work experience; to schemes involving the use of new technologies; or aiding recruitment to new, stable jobs or to self-employed activities. Schemes which come under either of these two main headings (long-term unemployed or youth integration) are looked at even more favourably when they are in one of the less developed areas of the European Community (Northern Ireland in the United Kingdom), one which has been affected by industrial decline or one in which rural development is being promoted (see under ss 3.2.1 for a list of such areas in the United Kingdom). Schemes may also attract funding when they involve two or more member states, training in advanced technology, innovation, modernisation, improved training structures, or integration into the labour market of disabled people, women (in occupations where they have been under-represented), and migrant workers (where they have been in the country for less than three years and need training).

Community initiatives

Three substantial 'human resource' initiatives have been funded in Great Britain solely through the ESF during the period 1991–4. These were the NOW (New Opportunities for Women: see chapter 5), HORIZON (for people with disabilities and those who are socially disadvantaged, see chapter 7) and EUROFORM (the development of new skills and qualifications). EUROFORM is aimed at the long-term unemployed, apprentices, young people and those threatened by unemployment. These three initiatives are likely to continue in some form after 1994 as part of a social exclusion programme.

The central aim of the Community initiatives is the transfer of knowledge and expertise between member states, primarily to those regions which are 'lagging behind' (Objective 1 regions). All projects must therefore have at least one partner in another member state and in addition must test out an innovatory approach in an area covered by the initiatives. Funds were fully committed over a year in advance before the end of the initiatives, and building transnational links always takes a great deal of time, so any preparations should be made promptly.

Applying for money

This section describes the arrangements for Great Britain. In Northern Ireland similar but different arrangements are in force and voluntary organisations in Northern Ireland are advised to consult the Northern Ireland Council of Voluntary Action for up-to-date details.

The ESF will support 'eligible' expenses. This covers most running costs but not building or any other capital costs. Organisations that want European Social Fund support for their activities must work through the nominated bodies who represent the social partners. Those of interest to the voluntary sector are the Industrial Common Ownership Movement, Vassali House, 20 Central Road, Leeds LS1 6DE, tel: 0532-461738; Women's Training Network, Aizelwoods Mill, Nursery Street, Sheffield S3 8GG, Tel: 0742-823172; and, more generally, NCVO (contact Chris Evans, NCVO, Regent's Wharf, 8 All Saints Street, London N1 9RL, Tel: 071-713 6161; Fax: 071-713 6300). NCVO has established a National Advisory Committee with regional and national representatives to give guidance for this. These bodies have devised techniques for assessing how the applications they receive from projects compare with the European Social Fund priorities. These are set out in a community support framework and more detailed operational programmes. After this comparison has been made the bodies will submit recommendations for funding to the Department of Employment who will scrutinise applications and issue approval where eligible. These selection criteria have been endorsed by appropriate monitoring committees.

The European Parliament is pressing for simplified management procedures and more controls over spending. The existing European Council regulations for implementing Structural Fund programmes in member states are due to expire on 31 December 1993. During 1993 consultation between the European Commission and member states will take place, with new regulations and priorities for assistance being due to come into effect on 1 January 1994.

3.4.2 Action and research on the labour market

ERGO is a Commission action research programme with a total budget of around 1.5 million ecu, which has been designed to identify successful programmes and projects which will benefit long-term unemployed people. Small amounts of money are available on an annual basis which are mainly for research and seminars but also for local employment initiatives such as co-operatives. Current main interests are local employment development and long-term unemployment. The purpose is to help develop European Community policy and priorities. Projects must have a European Community slant or be conducted simultaneously in different countries. An example of past research funded was a study on workers' co-operatives by the Mutual Aid Centre. Write to John Morley or Danny Brennan (both British) responsible for employment and labour market policy in Directorate-General V, Commission of the European Communities, Rue de la Loi 200, 1049 Brussels, tel: 010 32 2 295 1098. ERGO News is available from DG V on request.

3.4.3 Local and regional employment creation

The Commission and the International Union of Local Authorities have recently established a special support programme for employment creation. This provides financial support for innovatory projects linked to changes in employment. Applications should be made to (and information obtained from) the International Union of Local Authorities, PO Box 90646, 2509 LP The Hague, Netherlands, Tel: 010 31 32 7032 44032; Fax: 010 31 37 7032 46916.

3.4.4 Local Employment Development Action Programme

The Commission runs a Local Employment Development Action Programme (LEDA) with a small annual budget of 1 million ecu. This is an experimental action and research programme drawing on successful local responses to employment problems in selected districts where unemployment is particularly high. These districts include Nottingham and Dundee. Further information may be obtained from LEDA, South Bank Technopark, London Road, London SE1 6LN, tel: 071-922 8835; Fax: 071-261 1166.

3.4.5 European System of Documentation on Employment (SYSDEM)

SYSDEM is another Commission-supported activity. It collects information and provides interpretation and advice. For further information contact John Penny, Ecotec Research and Consulting Ltd, 25 Square de Meeus, 1040 Brussels, Tel: 010 32 2 511 2058; Fax: 010 32 2 511 2522.

3.4.6 European Regional Development Fund (ERDF)

Since the reform of the fund in 1988, grant aid in the assisted and other areas takes the following forms:

(i)   regional operational programmes including those originated by the member state (formerly National Programmes of Community Interest), those from Community initiatives (formerly Community Programmes, eg RESIDER – declining steel areas, RENAVAL – declining shipbuilding areas, RECHAR – declining coal-mining areas), and integrated approaches involving the use of more than one structural fund;
(ii)   part-financing of national aid schemes;
(iii) provision of global grants managed by an intermediary in the member state;
(iv)   part-financing of major projects; and
(v)   support for technical assistance and studies in preparation of programmes.

Most UK programmes will fall into the first of these categories. Programmes will contain projects, but these collectively will have to form a coherent programme.

The Committee of the Regions has been set up to act as a consultancy body on matters which impinge on the regions. Its term of office is four years and it is composed of 189 representatives of local and regional authorities. The UK, France, Germany and Italy each have 24 representatives on the committee, Spain has 21, Belgium, Greece, the Netherlands and Portugal have 12, Denmark and Ireland have 9 and Luxembourg has 6. The UK's representatives are to be elected.

The Commission has proposed an increased flexibility in the allocation of funds to areas excluded from Objectives 1, 2 and 5b. Structural funds for Objective 1 regions have been estimated at 96.3 billion ecu for the period 1994–9.

Under the old rules, organisations helping small and medium-sized businesses to develop local potential may receive funding for advice, research and support work. Special aid has been available for areas affected by decline in the steel, shipbuilding and textile industries. Community and national programmes and project financing all provide multi-annual assistance, amounting to up to 50 per cent of eligible expenditure. This includes schemes which aid industry, craft industries, services or infrastructure investment. Schemes costing less than £30,000 are not normally considered. In ss 3.2.2 we have described the new objectives for the work of all the structural funds. The ERDF covers Objectives 1, 2 and 5b. Objective 1 is for the development of disadvantaged regions of which Northern Ireland is the only designated region in the United Kingdom. Objective 2 is for the conversion of regions affected by industrial decline of which there are many eligible areas in the United Kingdom (see ss 3.2.1 for a broad description of these areas). More specific details can be obtained from Jane Duck, Department of Trade and Industry, Room 232, Kingsgate House, 66 Victoria Street, London SW1E 6SW, Tel: 071-215 8594.

Applications are predominantly in the form of operational programmes. They have to be included in regional plans submitted to the Commission. From the plans the Commission draws up Community Support Frameworks (CSFs) which set out their intentions for ERDF support in the eligible areas. Support is then allocated to operational programmes arising out of the CSFs.

Project financing

The types of project for which the government may receive aid fall into two main categories: industrial, tourist and service activities; and infrastructure projects. ERDF regulations allow the grants to be passed on to the project concerned or to be held back by the government as partial reimbursement of state aid. In practice the government takes the second option and uses the resources it saves to assist additional projects. In this way fund assistance is used not to increase the value of the aid given to individual projects but, it is claimed, to increase the number of projects which receive aid.

Industrial, tourist and service activities

Eligible projects in this area should create or preserve jobs. Typically, assistance is given for the construction of new workshops and the establishment of advice centres. Leisure and sports facilities, parks, public libraries, museums, theatres, cultural and conference centres and cultural heritage projects must be linked to the promotion of tourism to receive aid. Govan Workspace received funds under RENAVAL to refurbish former shipbuilding premises and create 23 workspace units for small businesses.

Infrastructure projects

Projects eligible for assistance include roads, gas, electricity and water supply, research and development facilities and the construction of 'advance' factories (which encourage industrial development). Public administration buildings, old people's and nursing homes, the building and renovation of housing and coastal and soil protection with an exclusively agricultural bias are all specifically excluded from funding. Hospitals and general education establishments are excluded except in Northern Ireland. The Commission, however, proposes to give investment in health and education more help in future.

Community initiatives

Measures qualifying for assistance under Community initiatives can provide a better link between the Community's objectives for structural development or conversion of regions and the objectives of other Community policies. They typically concern a region or regions in more than one member state. The establishment of new economic activities in areas of high unemployment in declining areas is usually the main objective. Aid is sometimes allowed outside the United Kingdom's assisted areas, but this is exceptional. A recent example is the funding of some pilot actions in depressed parts of London. The objectives of this scheme are to introduce economic activity into public housing estates, restore derelict land, extend employment opportunities to local communities and develop the economic potential for ethnic minorities.

RETEX

RETEX is a new fund, with a budget of 500 million ecu for the period 1993-8, which will help regions which are heavily dependent on the textiles and clothing sector. Of the aid 90% is earmarked for Objective 1 regions and the remainder for regions covered by Objectives 2 and 5(b). Northern Ireland is to receive 2.6 million ecu. The sort of schemes likely to attract support include those to improve know-how, design and quality control, help to set up local business groups, training schemes and the rehabilitation of waste land and redundant buildings.

Studies and consultancy work

Studies closely related to the operations of the Regional Fund, and initiated by the Commission, may receive 50-70 per cent or, very exceptionally, 100 per cent funding. Studies or projects which help small or medium-sized firms to expand, develop local potential and gain access to new technology and the capital market may receive up to 50-70 per cent funding. More information on eligible projects is available from the Department of Trade and Industry.

Who can apply?

Private individuals and companies benefit indirectly from the ERDF as the anticipated receipts increase the level of money available for regional aid. Applications for regional aid should be directed to the regional offices of the Department of Trade and Industry, the Industry Department of Scotland, the Welsh Office Industrial Department or the Department of Economic Development for Northern Ireland, as appropriate (addresses below). These departments claim back money paid out to projects that are eligible for Fund support from the Commission. Public and local authorities in England make application for aid through the specified contact points and local offices of the Department of the Environment, given on the DoE application form. In Scotland, Wales and Northern Ireland applications are made to the departments named above. These departments will give advice and guidance and select projects which are eligible for fund support. The Commission makes the ultimate decision on which projects are eligible to receive aid from the structural funds, although it will consult extensively with the member states and regional authorities concerned, in the spirit of 'partnership'. In general, it can be said that the Regional Fund will aim (as it always has) at helping to redress the principal imbalances between the different regions in the Community by assisting those whose economic development is lagging behind or has declined or needs (as in some rural areas) the substitution of new enterprise. Aid from the fund will continue to be applied through central government and operated largely by local authorities. Emphasis on employment, enterprise, technology and research will be looked on favourably.

Addresses for applications

Anne O'Sullivan
Department of the Environment
2 Marsham Street
London SW1P 3EB

Industry Department for Scotland
New St Andrew's House
St James' Centre
Edinburgh EH1 3TA

Welsh Office
Cathays Park
Cardiff CF1 3NQ

Department of Economic
Development for Northern Ireland
Arches Centre
11/13 Bloomfield Avenue
Belfast BT5 5HD

Department of Trade and Industry
North Eastern Region
Stanegate House
2 Groat Market
Newcastle upon Tyne NE1 1YN

Yorkshire and Humberside Region
Priestly House
Park Row
Leeds LS1 5LF

North Western Region
Sunley Building
Piccadilly Plaza
Manchester M1 4BA

Merseyside Sub Office
Graeme House
Derby Square
Liverpool L2 7UP

East Midlands Region
Severns House
20 Middle Pavement
Nottingham NG1 7DW

West Midlands Region
Ladywood House
Stephenson Street
Birmingham B2 4DT

South West Region
Pithay
Bristol BS1 2PB

3.4.7 European Centre for the Development of Vocational Training (CEDEFOP)

Research projects or seminars just might get funding from this European Community quango set up in 1975 as a centre for discussion, research, information and exchange of experience among industry, trade unions, governments and the Commission in the field of vocational training. Its current interests include youth, equal opportunities for men and women, migrant workers, people with disabilities, technological development and qualifications, vocational training, regional development and job creation programmes, the training of trainers and training structures and systems. Activities are organised around four-year programmes which implement their priority themes by annual work programmes. Although its statutes allow for pilot projects, its budget currently confines it to the organisation of conferences and the commissioning of research. Voluntary organisations are not represented on its management board so they tend not to be invited to seminars etc. Generally, research commissions are given to academic institutions. It is up to you, therefore, to make the first approach and to show how you can help with CEDEFOP's work. If you are interested, obtain copies of the latest *CEDEFOP Action Guidelines* and annual work programme and look for areas of common interest. Contact the Director, CEDEFOP, Jean Monnet House, Bundasallee 22, D-1000 Berlin 15, Germany, Tel: 010 49 30 88 41 20. CEDEFOP also organises study visits for training specialists (see ss 9.4.3). Working in close collaboration with CEDEFOP is the newly established European Training Foundation. Its role will be to assure effective co-operation in the implementation of assistance to the countries of central and eastern Europe in the field of vocational training.

3.4.8 European Foundation for the Improvement of Living and Working Conditions

The Foundation is a similar body to CEDEFOP but with the different area of work which its name implies. Living conditions of the long-term unemployed are included in its programme. For more details see ss 11.5.6.

3.4.9 Youth Initiative Projects

Partnership in Training and Research (PETRA), the action programme for the vocational training of young people in their preparation for adult and working life, awards grants of up to £6,000 for young people's projects creating employment, devising training programmes, developing their own information systems and enabling participation in social and cultural activities (see ss 9.4.1).

3.4.10 Training in new technology

Help for individuals undergoing training, and for organisations running or developing training in new technologies, is available under Co-operation between Universities and Enterprises on Training in the Field of Technology (COMETT). See ss 9.4.2.

3.4.11 Training for the employed

FORCE surveys and forecasts future demands for skills, occupations and qualifications through partnership arrangements and international exchange schemes lasting one to two years. The maximum grant for large projects is 200,000 ecu and 7,500 for exchanges. Further information from FORCE, rue du Nord 34, 1,000 Brussels, Tel: 010 32 2 209 1311; Fax: 010 32 2 209 1320.

3.5 Key publications

Full information and documentation on the European Social Fund is available from NCVO and details from Ulric White: Regent's Wharf, 8 All Saints Street, London N1 9RL, Tel: 071-713 6161; Fax: 071-713 6300

1992 The Social Dimension, EC, Periodical 2/1990, European documentation, available from the Commission's information office, 8 Storey's Gate, London SW1P 3AT, Tel: 071-973 1992; Fax: 071-973 1900

Annual guide to ESF applicants, Department of Employment, ESF Section, 236 Grays Inn Road, London WC1X 8HL, Tel: 071-211 4732; Fax: 071-211 4749

Europe in Britain, examples of Structural fund expenditure in Britain, available from European Parliament UK Office, 2 Queen Anne's Gate, London SW1H 9AA, Tel: 071-222 0411; Fax: 071-222 2713

Helping Europe's Regions, and *Working for the Regions*, Europe on the Move series, obtainable free from the Commission's information offices, 8 Storey's Gate, London SW1P 3AT, Tel: 071-973 1992; Fax: 071-973 1900

Operations of the European Community concerning Small and Medium-sized Enterprises, practical handbook, Commission of the European Community, available from HMSO

Pickup bulletin and *Europe's money: a guide to the budget of the European Communities, 1991*, from the Pickup Europe unit, South Bank Polytechnic, Borough Rd, London SE1 0AA, Tel: 071-633 9249; Fax: 071-261 9426. Pickup Europe works with Training and Enterprise Councils (TECs) to help industry cope with the Single Market

The Social Challenge, EC, Europe on the Move series, available free from the Commission's information offices, 8 Storey's Gate, London SW1H 9AA, Tel: 071-222 0411; Fax: 071-222 2713

Social Europe, EC Commission, 3 issues per year, subscription 50 ecu per year. Orders to the EC publications office, L-2985 Luxembourg

4 Poverty, Families and Elderly People

This chapter will be of interest primarily to voluntary organisations and professional bodies concerned with the welfare of families or tackling poverty and the problems of disadvantaged groups within Britain or within the European Community, as well as to housing associations (see ss 4.4.4), local authorities and trade unions. For poverty related to unemployment, see chapter 3.

4.1 Key Commission department

Employment, Social Affairs: Directorate-General V

Commissioner: Padraig Flynn (Irish)
Acting Director-General: Hywel Jones

Key officials: Odile Quintin, (French, speaks English), Tel: 010 32 2 299 2277; Dorangela van Loo-Lucioni, poverty programme (Italian, speaks English), Tel: 010 32 2 295 6489; Eamon McInerney, EC programme for older people (Irish), Tel: 010 32 2 299 0494; Fax: 010 32 2 299 0509, and Michèle Teirlinck family questions (French, speaks English) Tel: 010 32 2 299 2279. All of these officials work in the division dealing with social security and social action.

4.2 Extent of Community involvement

The major area of work is the programme on the 'economic and social integration of the economically and socially least privileged groups in society' – commonly known as Poverty 3. Previous programmes ran in 1975–80 and 1985–9. The present programme is for the period 1989–94 (see ss 4.4.1) and Poverty 4 is now under discussion. Article 118 of the

Treaty of Rome requires the Commission to promote close co-operation between member states in the social field, but the context makes it clear that this is largely related to the world of work and the Treaty base for action projects on poverty is slim. Article 2 requires the European Community to promote an accelerated raising of the standard of living, and the Single European Act and Maastricht Treaty call for greater 'social cohesion', but even the Social Chapter concentrates on employment issues.

The Commission has been anxious to extend its role in the field of poverty, arguing that the Community's economic policies have social consequences, for which it should take responsibility, and that national social measures affect competition. The Council has, on the other hand, been wary of creating a precedent for extra expenditure. In the past, poverty programmes have needed unanimous approval in the Council. Approval first came in 1975 as a follow-up to the famous 1972 pledge to give the Community a human face.

In addition to the work on poverty, the Community has agreed to a programme of work on the problems of the family. This arises to a large extent from a continental (especially French) concern about falling birth rates. The activities include studies, seminars and a review of the effects that other European Community policies have upon the family.

The year 1993 has been designated the European Year of Older People and Solidarity between the Generations. The aims of the year are to raise awareness of the issues of ageing, to emphasise the place of older people in the Community and promote positive images, to forge closer relationships between the generations and to facilitate the exchange of experience and practice across Europe.

4.3 Key people

4.3.1 In Britain

Dr Nick Buckley, Department of Social Security, Room 921, Adelphi, 1–11 John Adam Street, London WC2N 6HT, Tel: 071-962 8411

Professor Graham Room, Director of the Centre for Research in European Social and Employment Policy, University of Bath, Claverton Down, Bath BA2 7AY, Tel: 0225-826826. Graham Room was deeply involved in the evaluation of the first two poverty programmes. He is now the co-ordinator for the European Commission's observatory on social exclusion.

Katherine Duffy, The Local Government Centre, Warwick Business School, University of Warwick, Coventry CV4 7AL, Tel: 0203-524109; Fax: 0203-524410. Contact for UK Research and Development Unit, EC programme to combat poverty.

Sarah William, International Federation of Social Workers, rue de l'Athénee 33, CH 1206 Geneva, Switzerland, Tel: 010 41 22 47 1236; Fax: 010 41 22 46 8657.

MEPs

Tom Megahy (Labour, Yorkshire South West, 3 Burton Street, Wakefield, West Yorkshire WF1 2DD, Tel: 0924-382396; Fax: 0924-366851) is a member of the Social Affairs Committee and has been its rapporteur on poverty questions. The co-chairs of the European Parliament Inter-Group on Ageing are Sir Jack Stewart Clark MEP and Hugh McMahon MEP.

4.3.2 At European Community level

COFACE is concerned with poverty as it affects families. British contacts: Jennie Pugh, NFWI, 104 New King's Road, London SW6, Tel: 071-371 9300; Fax: 071-716 3652
Bronwen Cohen, Children in Scotland, 55 Albany Street, Edinburgh, EH1 3QY, Tel: 031-288 8484; Fax: 031-228 8585

Michaela Bergman, Help the Aged International, 16–18 St James's Walk, London EC1R 0BE, Tel: 071-253 0253; Fax: 071-253 4814

Eurolink Age has members in all 12 member states and is concerned with ageing issues and the position of older people in society. Its work includes the effects of poverty. UK members are Age Concern England, Astral House, 1268 London Road, London SW16 4ER, Tel: 081-679 8000; Fax: 081-679 6069, and the British Society of Gerontology.

Ecumenical Commission for Church and Society, rue Joseph II 174, 1040 Brussels, Tel: 010 32 2 230 1732. Official representatives of Councils of Churches and churches in the 12 member states of the European Community (includes observer Roman Catholic members)

European Anti-Poverty Network, 205 rue Bélliard, Bte 13, 1040 Brussels, Tel: 010 32 2 230 4455; Fax: 010 32 2 230 9733. UK contacts are NCVO, the Scottish Council for Voluntary Organisations (SCVO), Wales Council for Voluntary Action (WCVA) and Northern Ireland Council for Voluntary Action.

Barbara and David Forbes, Quaker Council for European Affairs, 50 Square Ambiorix, 1040 Brussels, Tel: 010 32 2 230 4935

4.4 Funding

4.4.1 European Community poverty programmes

The first programme ran from 1975 to 1980 on a budget of about £12 million. Fifteen United Kingdon projects were 50 per cent funded with up to £200,000 allocated per project. They included both action-research projects to alleviate poverty directly by, for example, providing after-school care facilities to allow mothers to work, and advisory/welfare rights projects concerned with the causes of poverty. Voluntary agencies were heavily involved with the development of the programme. Most of the UK action projects were established and run by voluntary organisations.

The second programme ran from 1985 to 1989. It also included action-research projects but on a limited number of themes, covering long-term unemployed people, young unemployed people, homeless people, elderly people, single-parent families, refugees and migrant workers. The projects were mainly in either underprivileged urban areas or in impoverished rural areas. The European Community spent some £18 million on the second programme and the projects were expected to find half their funding from other sources. In the UK there were 17 action research projects covering most of the themes. A small amount of money is being spent in follow up programmes on some of the themes.

The third programme is supporting two kinds of projects. Prototype experiences [in the UK they are in Liverpool, Edinburgh and Brownlow (Northern Ireland)] bring together all the agencies concerned with poverty in a particular area. This is quite different from previous programmes which have depended to a large extent upon the voluntary sector. The involvement of new actors – especially local government – is welcome even if it reduces the amount of funding available to voluntary organisations. The second kind of project is reserved for specific initiatives by non-governmental organisations in favour of particular groups, for example, one-parent families co-ordinated from Bristol, former prisoners in Italy or reformed drug-users in Greece. The European Community intended to spend some 55 million ecu on this programme in the years 1989–94. This money is now allocated so the only way of getting access to funds is by involvement in one of the projects, which is only possible if you are in one of the designated areas. The fourth programme is expected to start soon after the current one ends, although a delay of a few months is possible. The shape of the programme is as yet undecided but early registration of your interest is advisable.

In addition to the projects, all three programmes have had an element of research, co-ordination and evaluation. This has created a body of literature and many suggestions for policy changes which would combat poverty.

Under the present programme these functions are being co-ordinated by 'A&R' the European Group for Economic Affairs and Research, 301 Rue Pierre le Grand, F59042 Cedex, Lille, France, Tel: 010 33 20 439 543; Fax: 010 33 20 333 515.

4.4.2 Meetings and studies on the family

A limited number of meetings of European Community-wide interest that concern the family are funded by Directorate-General V. DG V has a general budget for research which is devoted mainly to employment studies, but family issues are also eligible. Apply to DG V at the Commission's Brussels address.

4.4.3 First EC Programme for Older People

The first EC programme for older people runs from 1991 to 1993. This includes policy statements and funding for research studies and awareness-raising projects, leading up to the European Year of Older People and Solidarity between the Generations in 1993. Funding is given for events, research, exchange visits and projects involving more than one member state. The UK Core Programme has four themes: combating ageism, promoting health and active leisure, volunteering, and removing barriers to social and environmental integration. Contact June O'Connor, European Year of Older People 1993 UK Secretariat, c/o Age Concern England, Astral House, 1268 London Road, London, SW16 4ER, tel: 081-679 8000; Fax: 081-679 6069.

4.4.4 Aid for the housing of coal and steel workers

The European Coal and Steel Community provides loans at low rates of interest for the construction, purchase and modernisation of housing for workers in the two industries. Priority goes to projects associated with restructuring of the industries or benefiting workers with the worst living and working conditions. The projects of housing authorities, housing associations and the industries themselves, as well as the house purchase of some individual workers, are eligible for loans. Individuals should contact their personnel officer or trade union representative for more information; organisations should contact the ECSC housing committee for their industry. Antoon Herpels at the Brussels office of the European Commission, Tel: 010 32 2 295 1550, can provide information.

4.4.5 Free and subsidised food

The European Community makes some of the surplus food generated by the Common Agricultural Policy available to charities and non-profit making institutions.

Butter is available throughout the year at about half price to non-profit making institutions involved in education or caring such as schools, hospitals and old people's homes. Contact ext. 2647 of the Intervention Board, Tel: 0734-583626.

Certain fruit and vegetables may be withdrawn from the market and donated free to charities, prisons, hospitals, schools and people in receipt of public assistance. Transport will normally be arranged and paid for by recipients. Cauliflowers are generally only available in Lincolnshire, apples and pears in Kent. Tomatoes may occasionally also be available. Contact ext. 2907 of the Intervention Board, Tel: 0734-583626.

One of the methods available to fish producers for disposal of surplus is to have it withdrawn from the market and distributed free of charge, in its natural state, to recognised UK charitable societies or institutions. Fish is generally only available in Scotland and participation is at the discretion of the fish producer. Interested organisations should contact the producers directly.

There are now 1,367 charitable and non-profit making organisations designated to participate in a two-year Surplus Food Scheme running between April 1992 and March 1994. They distribute intervention stock which is surplus to requirements, currently butter and beef, to eligible beneficiaries. In the UK these have been defined as people on income support, those in receipt of family credit or disability working allowance, homeless and destitute, and people living in welfare hostels. Contact 0734-583626, ext. 2201.

For any further information contact the Intervention Board for Agricultural Produce, Fountain House, 2 Queens Walk, Reading RG1 7QW, Tel: 0734-583626.

4.4.6 Technology for Elderly and Disabled people: the TIDE and COST initiatives

See ss 7.4.2.

4.5 Key publications

Action Anti-Poverty Action-Research in Europe, by Graham Room, School of Advanced Urban Studies, Bristol, 1993

Age and Attitudes – main results from a Eurobarometer survey, available from the London Office of the Commission, 8 Storey's Gate, London SW1P 3AT, Tel: 071-973 1992; Fax: 071-973 1900

Behind the Statistics: profiles of older people in poverty from around Europe, 1992 (£5); *Welfare Pluralism, the voluntary sector and elderly people: east and west*, 1992 (£5); *EC programme for elderly people, one year on*, December 1991 (free); all available from Eurolink Age, Age Concern England, Astral House, 1268 London Road, London SW16 4ER, Tel: 081-679 8000; Fax: 081-679 6069

COFACE Contacts, monthly newsletter available on request from William Lay (see ss 13.3.2)

Communication examining the problem of social exclusion, COM (92) 542, December 1993, available from the London Office of the Commission, 8 Storey's Gate, London SW1P 3AT, Tel: 071-973 1992; Fax: 071-973 1900

Eurolink Age Bulletin, published three times per year, subscription details available from Eurolink Age, Age Concern England, Astral House, 1268 London Road, London SW16 4ER, Tel: 081-679 8000; Fax: 081-679 6069

European Networks of Innovative Projects Concerning Older People (a directory), European Commission, 200 Rue de la Loi, 1049, Brussels

Final Report on the Second European Programme to Combat Poverty 1985-1989, European Commission, Brussels, 1991

Network News, European Anti-Poverty Network, 205 rue Bélliard, Bte 13, 1040 Brussels, Tel: 010 32 2 230 4455; Fax: 010 32 2 230 9733

Observatory on National Policies to Combat Social Exclusion – Second Annual Report, by Graham Room, Published by European Economic Interest Group, 'Animation and Research', 60 Rue Jacquemars Gielle, 59800 Lille, France

Older People in Europe: Social and Economic Policies, the 1993 Report of the European Observatory, available from the London Office of the Commission, 8 Storey's Gate, London SW1P 3AT, Tel: 071-973 1992; Fax: 071-973 1900

Population and Social Conditions, Eurostat Rapid Reports, 1990

Research Problematics, ed by G. Abou Sada and N. Yeates, July 1991. Published by GEIE Animation & Research, 60 Rue Jacquemars Gielee, 59800 Lille, France

Windows of opportunity: public policy and the poor, Saul Becker (ed.), ISBN 0 946744 351, October 1991, £6.95 including P&P from Child Poverty Action Group Ltd, 1–5 Bath Street, London EC1V 9PY

5 *Women*

This chapter is of particular interest to women's organisations, trade unions and industry.

5.1 Key Commission departments

Employment, Industrial Relations and Social Affairs: Directorate-General V

Commissioner: Padraig Flynn

Acting Director-General: Hywel Jones

Key official: Agnes Hubert (French, speaks English), head of Equal Opportunities Unit, DG V B4, Tel: 010 32 2 295 9093

Audiovisual, Information: Directorate-General X

Commissioner: Joao Pinheiro

Director-General: Colette Flesche (Luxembourg), Tel: 010 32 2 299 9418

Key official: Anne-Blanche Haritos (speaks English), Tel: 010 32 2 299 9418; Ms Haritos heads the Women's Information Service.

5.2 Extent of Community involvement

European Community action is based on Article 119 of the Treaty of Rome, which provides that 'Each member state shall, during the first stage, ensure and subsequently maintain the application of the principle that men and women should receive equal pay for equal work.' Six European Community laws (directives) have been passed. The first applies the principle of equal pay; the second implements the principle of equal access to employment, vocational training and promotion; and the third makes a start towards equal treatment for men and women in social security matters. The fourth covered equal treatment in occupational social security schemes, the fifth equal treatment for self-employed men and women (including the protection of self-employed women during pregnancy and motherhood) and the sixth allowed women to take maternity leave of at least 14 weeks.

The third medium-term action programme is for the period 1991–5, and has three objectives: to implement and develop the law, to integrate women into the labour market, and to improve the status of women in society. It includes the reconciliation of working life with family responsibilities, providing information and raising awareness, achieving a positive image in the media, and participation in economic and social life.

As a result of the third medium-term Community Action Programme and its predecessor, European Community-wide networks have been set up covering implementation of legislation, positive action in businesses, women in the labour market, women in television, childcare, and other measures to reconcile work and family responsibilities, education, women in the decision making process, local employment initiatives and training schemes for women. This last network is known as IRIS. The Commission provides some of the funding necessary for the co-ordination of IRIS which is carried out by the Centre for Research in European Women (CREW) (see ss 5.3.2). The European Social Fund partially funds 34 per cent of IRIS activities. The networks are overseen by the Equal Opportunities Unit in DG V.

The Social Chapter covers equality between men and women as regards, in particular, access to employment, remuneration, working conditions, social protection, education, vocational training and career development. It also envisages the development of measures enabling men and women to reconcile their occupational and family obligations.

5.3 Key people

5.3.1 In Britain

Patricia-Anne Moore, NOW Co-ordinator, Northern Ireland University, Enterprise Training Partnership, Swinson House, Glenmount Road, Church Road, Newtonabbey, BT36 7LH, Tel: 0232-365171, ext 266; 0232-862912

Kenneth Munro at the Commission's Edinburgh office, 9 Alva Street, Edinburgh EH2 3AT, Tel: 031-225 2058; Fax: 031-226 4105

Lorraine Huggins, European Social Fund Unit, 11 Belgrave Road, London SW1V 1RB, Tel: 071-834 6644; Fax: 071-828 7041

Equal Opportunities Commission, Overseas House, Quay Street, Manchester M3 3HN, Tel: 061-833 9244

Holli Ball, National Alliance of Women's Organisations, 279-81 Whitechapel Road, London E1 1BY, Tel: 071-247 7052

Peter Moss, Thomas Coram Research Unit, 27 Woburn, London WC1H 0AA, Tel: 071-612 6954

Sue Bell, Women's Training Network, Aizelwoods Mill, Nursery Street, Sheffield S3 8GG, Tel: 0742-823172

MEPs
Christine Crawley (Labour, Birmingham East) who is the chair of the Parliament's Committee on Women's Rights, 16 Bristol Street, Birmingham B5 7AF, Tel: 021-622 2270

Margaret Daly (Conservative, Somerset and Dorset West), The Old School House, Aisholt, Spaxton, Bridgwater, Somerset TA5 1AR, Tel: 027867-688

For the names of other UK members of the Committee on Women's Rights see ss 1.2.2.

5.3.2 In Brussels

Centre for Research on Women (CREW), 21 rue de la Tourelle, 1040 Brussels, Tel: 010 32 2 230 5158. CREW is an independent co-operative producing a monthly bulletin and research studies on the European Community and women

European Women's Lobby, 22 rue du Meridien, 1030 Brussels, Tel: 010 32 2 217 9020

Committee of Family Organisations in the European Community (COFACE), rue de Londres 17, 1050 Brussels, Tel: 010 32 2 511 4179

The Advisory Committee on Equal Opportunities for Women and Men brings together the national equal opportunities and women's employment commissions to advise the European Commission in this field, UK Members: Kamlesh Bahl, chair, Equal Opportunities Commission and Joan Smith, chair, NI committee

5.4 Funding

5.4.1 Women and training

Women are eligible for all the schemes referred to in chapter 3 and have priority arrangements under the NOW initiative. The NOW (New Opportunities for Women) initiative was launched to achieve the objectives of the Third Action Programme for Equal Opportunities for Women. The aim was to give the structural funds a dimension of equality. It had a total budget of 153 million ecu over a period of three years (1990–3) from the European Social Fund to promote equal rights at work and in professional training. This will probably continue.

One particular vocational training scheme under the ESF was the Powys TEC's Synchro project. It was set up to help unemployed women into occupations where they are traditionally under-represented while at the same time supporting investment to benefit the local economy. The project provided training for the skills required to produce high quality wiring harnesses for Lucas at their recently established factory.

5.4.2 Projects and studies to promote equal opportunities

The women's section within DG V has a small annual budget to co-fund a variety of projects for organisations and individuals. Recent examples have included conferences and seminars, exchange visits between people from different member states, small projects designed to promote equal opportunities between women and men at a practical level, and, occasionally, research on subjects which fall within its current programme (see s 5.2).

There must be a European dimension to your project. All projects that get Commission support should be models of good practice which might act as an example to others. The Commission favours projects whose benefits are not confined to one organisation or group, but shared with those from other countries. But the most important criteria are innovation and excellence. The section works on a yearly budget so it is impossible to predict what the following year's allocation will be. The demand for funds has always been great. It is important, therefore, to apply early in the year in which your project is to start, or – even better – the year before. Application forms and further information is available from Agnes Hubert, DG V, at the Commission's Brussels address. Applications should make clear what your overall budget is, what other funds have been committed and how much the Commission is being asked to contribute. The Commission likes to support as wide a spectrum of projects as possible and so there is no guarantee of continuous funding for a project.

5.4.3 Grants for women setting up businesses

Local Employment Initiatives were started in 1984 to give grants to women setting up employment creation initiatives such as businesses or co-operatives. Innovative projects and areas of high unemployment are given priority. The budget amounts to about £1 million per year, with grants being allocated at an average rate of £1,000 per full-time job per year. The schemes should have between two and five women to qualify for grants, and important factors include the benefit that women would derive from employment, and the economic viability of the scheme. Contact Dr Patricia Richardson, Women's Enterprise Unit, SEF, University of Stirling, Stirling, FK9 4LA, Tel: 0786-467353/467348; Fax: 0786-450201; or Women's LEI Grants Management, Comitato Impresa Donna – CNA, 1 Avenue de la Joyeuse Entrée, 1040 Brussels, Tel: 010 32 2 280 0054/0992; Fax: 010 32 2 280 0901.

5.4.4 Education

Finance for projects to encourage equal treatment of girls in education and vocational training is available under the PETRA programme (see ss 9.4.1).

5.4.5 Women of Europe Award

Every year, the Women's Information Service sponsors the Woman of Europe Award. This is presented to a woman, or a group of women, in recognition of an outstanding voluntary contribution towards European Community integration, selected from 12 national winners. Contact Alison Parry, 158 Buckingham Palace Road, London, SW1W 9TR, Tel: 071-891 1021.

5.4.6 Women in development

See s 10.6.20.

5.5 Key publications

Bridging the Gap: Women and Employment, by Margaret Daly MEP, Target Europe Paper No. 3, available from the European Democratic Group, 2 Queen Anne's Gate, London SW1H 9AA

CREW Reports, published monthly by the Centre for Research on European Women, 21 rue de la Tourelle, 1040 Brussels: Tel: 010 32 2 230 5158

Equal Rights, Equal Opportunities: The European Community and Women, 20-page brochure from the Women's Information Service in DG X, Information, Communication and Culture, rue de la Loi 200, 1049 Brussels, Tel: 010 32 2 299 1111

Europe for Women, leaflet available from the London Office of the Commission, 8 Storey's Gate, London SW1P 3AT, Tel: 071-973 1992; Fax: 071-973 1900

Social Europe: Equal Opportunities for women and men, Commission of the European Communities publication 3/91, 202-page book from the EC publications office 2985 Luxembourg

Women in Partnership, a video cassette about women in the European Community, available on loan from the Commission's Edinburgh information office, 9 Alva Street, Edinburgh EH2 3AT, Tel: 031-225 2058; Fax: 031-226 4105

Women of Europe Newsletter, monthly; and supplements (Nos 28–35 cover television, agriculture, statistics, childcare, Hungary, the French Revolution, the Third Action Programme, and women's attitudes towards politics), all available free from the Women's Information Service, DG X, rue de la Loi 200, 1049 Brussels, Tel: 010 32 2 299 1111

Women's Rights and Equal Opportunities, fact sheet, available from the London Office of the Commission, 8 Storey's Gate, London SW1P 3AT, Tel: 071-973 1992, Fax: 071-973 1900

6 People from Ethnic Minority Groups

This chapter will be of interest to voluntary organisations, local authorities, housing associations, advisory organisations and trade unions.

6.1 Key Commission departments

Commissioner: Padraig Flynn (Irish)

Task force for Human Resources Education, Training and Youth.
Key official: Alexandrios Tsolakis (French), deals with the education of migrants' children, Tel: 010 32 2 295 9981

Employment, Industrial Relations and Social Affairs:
Directorate-General V.

Acting Director-General: Hywel Jones
Key official: Annette Bosscher (Dutch, speaks English), head of division dealing with migrants, Tel: 010 32 2 295 1052; Fax: 010 32 2 295 1899

6.2 Extent of Community involvement

Historically the European Community has had no activities specifically for people from ethnic minorities. Some of the work on migrant workers has, however, been used in ways which have been useful for ethnic minorities. Articles 48–51 of the Treaty of Rome provide for freedom of movement for workers and DG V's Action Programme in Favour of Migrant Workers and their Families covers free movement, social services, housing, children's education, health, information, statistics and civic and political rights. It applies to both Community migrants and migrants from outside the Community, with the sole exception of the right of free access to employment which is linked to European Community nationality.

A Parliamentary resolution of 1992 calls on the member states to offer the children of migrant workers the right to appropriate education in the language of the host country and urges member states to promote supplementary teaching of the mother tongues of the children.

The Community (led by the European Parliament) has become concerned about racism and xenophobia, especially racist attacks. In 1986 the Council, the Commission and the Parliament jointly signed a solemn declaration on the subject. The Parliament has an active Committee looking into racism and has called on the Commission to draw up a common action programme against racism. However, the Commission has no legal base to act on discrimination. Member states are preparing to take joint action on the admission of migrant workers from third countries and to determine visa policy together following adoption of the Maastricht treaty. The work so far has been carried out by a group whose main concerns are drug smuggling and terrorism, so there seems to be a risk that they will not have as a priority the civil rights of people who are legally moving about the European Community but who happen to be members of ethnic minorities. Lastly, it is an unfortunate fact that the Social Chapter makes no mention at all of the need to prevent racism in the workplace, though in its introduction to the action programme, which gives effect to the Social Chapter, the Commission stresses the need to eradicate discrimination based on race, colour or religion from the world of employment.

6.3 Key people

6.3.1 In Brussels

Jan Niessen, Churches' Committee for Migrants in Europe, 174 rue Joseph II, 1040 Brussels, Tel: 010 32 2 230 2011; Fax: 010 32 2 231 1413

6.3.2 In Britain

Anne Owers, Joint Council for the Welfare of Immigrants, 115 Old Street, London EC1V 9JR, Tel: 071-251 8706

Philip Rudge, European Consultation on Refugees and Exiles, Broadway House, 3–9 Broadway, London SW8 1ST, Tel: 071-582 6922

Paul Gordon, Runnymede Trust, 11 Princelet Street, London E1 6QH, Tel: 071-375 1496; Fax: 071-247 7695

The Refugee Forum, 54 Tavistock Place, London WC1, Tel: 071-482 3829
The forum is a self-help umbrella organisation with 56 branches in Britain.

MEPs

Glyn Ford (Labour, Greater Manchester East), 3 Market Place, Ashton-under-Lyne, Lancashire OL6 7JD, Tel: 061-344 3000

6.4 European Community funds

So far no funds have been allocated specifically for the concerns of ethnic minorities. The fund for humanitarian affairs (see s 8.4.1) has been used from time to time and is particularly concerned with information work on the dangers of racism and fascism.

6.4.1 Organisations assisting migrant workers

Directorate-General V has a small annual budget for organisations offering help to migrants. General assistance, reception services and the provision of information and courses are all activities which are eligible for funding. As this is only a small budget, its aim is to give temporary help, for instance to get a project started, after which it should become self-supporting. You will need to obtain the appropriate application form and information note from Directorate-General V and return with the requested information on the proposed activities/project and on your organisation. Since the budget is annual, the directorate does not know how much money it has to spend until the beginning of the year. The best time to apply is at the end of the preceding year. Write to Annette Bosscher at the Commission, rue de Loi 200, 1049 Brussels.

6.4.2 Training and education

Special provision is made for migrant children under the PETRA programme (see ss 9.4.1). In the past the European Social Fund has been able to help vocational training programmes for migrant workers (see ss 3.4.1).

6.4.3 Housing

Grants are available to increase the supply of suitable housing for migrant workers and their families. Aid may go to the construction of new, and the adaptation of existing, accommodation; emergency accommodation for the homeless; and to housing services. In all cases a report must be made on the completion of the project. It helps if projects are innovatory (for example, in respect of target group, area, design, co-ordination), applicable elsewhere in the European Community, designed to promote social integration (by, for example, co-ordinating with other services such as work, leisure, vocational training) and guaranteed to be financially viable both in terms of capital and running costs, by a national or local government financial commitment.

Projects need not help migrants exclusively. Shelter has received money, for example, for a short-life housing project to benefit people who were not in the conventional housing market, including, in particular, migrant workers from southern Europe.

The available budget is small but there is no limit set for the European Community contribution to individual projects. The projects are normally selected in two phases, after 1 April and after 1 October. For further information, write to Annette Bosscher, Directorate-General V, at the Commission's Brussels address.

6.5 Key publications

Europe and Poverty, due to be published late in 1993 by Child Poverty Action Group Ltd, £6.95 including p&p from CPAG, 1–5 Bath Street, London EC1V 9PY

European Manifesto, available from Refugee Forum, 54 Tavistock Place, London WC1, Tel: 071-482 3829

Guide to EC Activities Relevant to Migrant and Refugee Communities, available from Refugee Forum, 54 Tavistock Place, London WC1, Tel: 071-482 3829

Immigration and Employment, EC Commission paper, 1992, available from the Commission's information offices, 8 Storey's Gate, London SW1P 3AT, Tel: 071-973 1992; Fax: 071-973 1900

Migration Newssheet, published by the Churches Committee for Migrants in Europe, 174 Rue Joseph II, 1040 Brussels

Race Equality, Europe and 1992, available free from the Commission for Racial Equality, Eliot House, 10–12 Allington Street, London SW1E 5EH, Tel: 071-828 7022

Refugee Charter, available from Refugee Forum, 54 Tavistock Place, London WC1, Tel: 071-482 3829

7 *People with Disabilities*

This chapter is intended for voluntary organisations, local authorities, trade unions and industry.

7.1 Key Commission department

Employment, Industrial Relations and Social Affairs:
Directorate-General V
Commissioner: Padraig Flynn (Irish)
Acting Director-General: Hywel Jones
Key official: Bernhard Wehrens (German, speaks English), responsible for action in favour of disabled people, Tel: 010 32 2 295 5039; Fax: 010 32 2 295 1012.
HELIOS office DG V.C4, 79 Avenue de Cortenberg, 1040 Brussels, Tel: 010 32 2 735 4105; Fax: 010 32 2 735 1671

7.2 Extent of Community involvement

The Treaty promises free movement of European Community citizens and commits the Community to involvement in the fields of employment, vocational training and social security. The Single European Act (see s 1.5.1) provides also for directives to ensure the health and safety of workers. In February 1993, the Council of Ministers adopted the HELIOS II programme which will run until December 1996, with a budget of approximately 37 million ecu. It focuses on: functional rehabilitation, integration into the educational system, vocational training and employment rehabilitation, economic integration, social integration and an independent way of life. The programme also includes the technical aides module of HANDYNET, a computerised, multilingual information system on disability questions.

HANDYNET enables information collected by member states to be exchanged, updated and adapted for use at a Community level, in order to offer a free service to people with disabilities. It includes a multi-lingual data base, electronic newspaper and computer-based message system. The technical aids module gives information on the aids available throughout the Community such as prices, manufacturers and distributors, and national procedures for obtaining the aids.

HELIOS II aims to improve co-ordination between disability programmes in member states, increase co-operation with European disability organ-isations and national councils of people with disabilities with the help of the European Disability Forum, harmonise its activities with the EC's HORIZON and TIDE initiatives, encourage the participation of people with disabilities in other Community programmes, and to promote awareness and make information more available.

In addition, the education of children with special needs is one of the priority themes within the Commission's study visit programme for educationalists: important concerted actions concerning sensory and physical disabilities are included in the Community's programme of medical research and there are projects about people with disabilities in various programmes to promote research and development of new technologies.

The EC transport division has started a pilot project on transport information for travellers with disabilities. They have drawn up a provisional checklist of information to be included in guides for people with disabilities; they also have an EC network of consultant specialists now active in information exchange between member states, with the aim of working towards an EC-wide information service for drivers with disabilities.

7.3 Key people

Bert Massey, the Royal Association for Disability and Rehabilitation (RADAR), 25 Mortimer Street, London W1N 8AB, Tel: 071-637 5400; Fax: 071-637 1827.

Tony Lumley, Mobility International, 228 Borough High Street, London SE1 1JX, Tel: 071-403 5688; Fax: 071-378 1292

Rachel Hurst, Disabled People's International European Community Committee, 11 Belgrave Road, London SW1V 1RB, Tel: 071-834 0477

John Thorne, MACINTYRE, 602 South Seventh Street, Milton Keynes, Bucks, Tel: 0908 262056

Arthur Jones, Department of Health, Alexander Fleming House, Room B1509, London SE1 6BY, Tel: 071-407 5522, ext 6647; Fax: 071-407 7154

HELIOS FORUM
Michael Barrett, UK HELIOS FORUM, 2 Tenterden Road, London N17 8BE, Tel: 081-808 6030; Fax 081-885 3235

Susan Parker-Scott, Employers' Forum on Disability, c/o Midland Bank, 3 Lower Thames Street, London EC3R 6HA, Tel: 071-321 6591

HELIOS Consultative Committee – UK Representatives
Trevor Boyle
Mobility International and PHAB
Northern Ireland
25 Alexandra Gardens
Belfast BT15 3LJ
Tel: 0232-370240

Glynis Phillips/Margaret Lowry
Department of Health
Health Care (A) 2D
Room 332
Wellington House
133–155 Waterloo Road
London SE1 8UG
Tel: 071-972 2000

Roy Kettle/Jenny Rigden
Department of Employment
SEPC3
Room 458
Caxton House
Tothill Street
London SW1H 9NF
Tel: 071-273 3000

MEP
Derek Prag (Conservative), Euro-Centre, Maynard House, The Common, Hatfield, Hertfordshire, Tel: 07072-71860. Mr Prag chairs the Parliament's Inter-group on Disability.

7.4 Funding

7.4.1 HELIOS II programme

Exchange and information activities between member states

The European Commission may contribute to activities between member states when these are concerned with the five areas of the HELIOS II programme (see s 7.2). Suitable activities are conferences, seminars, information exchanges, study visits and training courses. These should be arranged using annual topics agreed after consultation with the Committee. The Community will fund up to 50 per cent of the cost for conferences and up to 100 per cent for the other activities.

Co-operation with NGO

The Commission will formulate an annual programme of activities which are eligible for its support with appropriate priority ratings. These will include (in addition to the European-scale activities listed above) information to NGOs on Community-level actions, advice to the Commission on technical aspects when requested, and submission of an annual report on activities conducted within HELIOS II. Funding can be given for up to 50 per cent of costs for European-scale co-operative activities and up to 100 per cent for expenses of providing co-ordination and expertise.

Co-ordination with international activities

The programme aims to co-ordinate activities undertaken by organisations at an international level and to co-operate with other international activities. The following areas are included: functional rehabilitation, educational integration, vocational training and employment rehabilitation, economic and social integration and independent living.

Information and awareness-raising

The programme seeks to inform and raise awareness of the general public and the media, encouraging the integration of people with disabilities. This will involve activities and campaigns, and the Commission intends to organise competitions offering prizes to model projects concerning functional rehabilitation, education, training and employment, new technologies and technical aids and independent living. National meetings between HELIOS II participants to exchange information may also be funded. The Community will fund up to 100 per cent of activities' costs.

Special themes

All the above measures should give particular attention to prevention of, and early assistance in, impairments, incapacities and disabilities; difficulties faced by women with disabilities and older people, and by the families of people with disabilities; economic and social integration of women with disabilities; training for professionals and volunteers involved with integration; and people responsible for children with disabilities, adolescents and adults.

Further information is available from Nicola Bedlington, Tel: 010 32 2 295 5039; Fax: 010 32 2 295 1012.

7.4.2 Technology for Disabled and Elderly people: the TIDE and COST initiatives

The focus of TIDE (Technology Initiative for Disabled and Elderly People) is to find pragmatic technical solutions that enable and empower disabled and/or elderly people. TIDE is a user-focused programme concentrating on the application of existing technology to the needs of disabled and older people. The programme consists of 21 different action-projects under five different headings: (i) general models and tools; (ii) manipulation and control; (iii) personal communication; (iv) safety and daily support; and (v) access to information. It promotes the manufacture of special products and the adaptation of others of benefit to elderly and disabled people; it has established a permanent R&D structure for rehabilitation technology in Europe; it assists the co-ordination, balance and strengthening of the European market in rehabilitation technology products; it encourages standardisation in the field of rehabilitation technology; and it improves the quality and cost-effectiveness of technical aids for older people and people with disabilities. The initiative involves small and medium-sized enterprises, universities and other bodies. The TIDE programme has recently initiated a study in rehabilitation technology called HEART (Horizontal European Activities in Rehabilitation Technology). This started in April 1993 and will run for 18 months and will cover *inter alia* service delivery and training. TIDE have recently launched a newsletter. The TIDE initiative and the HELIOS II programme are co-ordinated as regards the HANDYNET system.

Further information can be obtained from Mr Egidio Ballabio, DG XIII/D/1 at the Commission's Brussels address, Tel: 010 32 2 299 0232; Fax:010 32 2 299 0248.

COST is a programme specifically aimed at the needs of older people and those with reduced mobility. It is not clear yet what level of political support there is for such a programme. For further information contact DG VII, Commission of the European Communities, 200 Rue de la Loi, Brussels.

7.4.3 HORIZON initiative

This Community initiative is geared to improving the conditions of access to the employment market for people with disabilities and disadvantaged persons, increasing their competitiveness. It finances local training initiatives and schemes providing help in finding employment with funds from the European Social Fund. It is therefore subject to the review of the Structural Funds (see chapter 3) but is likely to continue in some form after 1994. Applications for 1994 must include a transnational link, with at least one part of the project in an Objective 1 area. Pilot projects enabling infrastructures to be adapted to the needs of marginalised sections of society are financed in **Objective 1** regions covered by the European Regional Development **Funds**. Transnational networks are being established to transfer knowledge and experience to disadvantaged regions. It provides financial assistance for local innovative integration activities not covered by the HELIOS budget. The budget for 1991–3 was 180 million ecu, with a reinforcement in 1992 of 111.3 million ecu. Applications follow social fund procedures. Contact Mr Bernard Van der Haeghen (Belgian), Tel: 010 32 2 295 3975; Fax: 010 32 2 296 6280 and Natalie Pryer at NCVO, Tel: 071-713 6161.

7.4.4 Education

The education of children with special needs is an eligible theme within the programme to support the European activities of NGOs described in ss 7.4.1, and is a priority topic in the Study Visit Scheme for Educationalists (ARION). See section 9.4.3.

7.4.5 Prevention, early detection of disease and rehabilitation

The European Community finances the co-ordination of medical and public health research as part of its research programme, BIOMED 1. Past programmes have included disabilities, specifically congenital abnormalities, ageing and diseases, thrombosis, multiple sclerosis and diabetes. Prevention, care and health systems have had 27.5 million ecu allocated for 1994–8. See ss 12.4.2 for more information. The European Community also provides up to 60 per cent funding for projects in the fields of medicine, safety, hygiene and ergonomics in the coal and steel industries.

7.4.6 Support for sports events for people with disabilities

The Commission provides money for sports events with a European dimension for people with disabilities. Events should involve disabled participants from at least four of the member states and should raise public awareness of their sporting abilities as well as promoting the EC. Grants generally range from £1,500 to £15,000. Applications should be made to the British Paralympics Association, Room G13A, Delta Point, 35 Wellesley Road, Croydon, Surrey, CR9 2YZ, Tel: 081-666 4556; Fax: 081-666 4617.

7.4.7 Cultural projects involving people with disabilities

See under ss 9.5.2

7.5 Key publications

Council Decision of 25 February 1993 establishing a third Community action programme to assist disabled people (1993–6) (OJ L 56/30-9/3/1993), available from the London Office of the Commission, 8 Storey's Gate, London SW1P 3AT, Tel: 071-973 1992; Fax: 071-973 1900

TIDE Newsletter, The Swedish Handicap Institute, Box 510, S-162 15 Vallingby, Sweden

8 Human Rights

This chapter will be of interest to human rights organisations and to other voluntary organisations with an interest in social justice.

8.1 Key Commission departments

Legal Service
Director-General: Jean-Louis Dewost.

Secretariat General
Secretary General: David Williamson (British).

Key officials: Daniela Napoli (speaks English), deals with grants, Tel: 010 32 2 295 5501; Fax: 010 32 2 295 7850. Bourges Manoury, Tel: 010 32 2 295 2160/6480.

8.2 Extent of Community involvement

Human rights as such are not mentioned in the Treaty of Rome though provision is made for certain specific rights, notably for equal pay between men and women. The preamble to the Single European Act mentions the Council of Europe's European Convention on Human Rights and its Social Charter. The possibility of the European Community as such becoming a party to the European Convention on Human Rights is aired from time to time. The Community also increasingly raises the issue of human rights in its aid and trade negotiations with the countries of the South.

The European Parliament takes a keen interest in human rights questions both within the Community and in other countries. In 1988 a Belgian MEP called Karel de Gucht edited a comprehensive White Paper on the fundamental rights and freedoms of European citizens. This brought together the existing information on the legal status of a wide range of fundamental rights. A declaration of fundamental rights and freedoms was adopted in April 1989. This was followed by another resolution in July 1991 which called for the Community to accede to the European Convention on Human Rights. All European Community member states are party to the convention, but they vary in their acceptance of the provision for individuals to appeal to the bodies which uphold the rights listed in the convention. The Parliament's Committee on Petitions frequently raises questions relating to the human rights of European Community citizens. The Political Affairs Committee has a sub-committee which produces an annual report on the status of human rights around the world. Resolutions on human rights are a feature of all plenary sessions of the Parliament. There is also much concern about racism and xenophobia; see chapter 6.

For many years the member states have attempted to align their foreign policies. Under Maastricht, police and judicial co-operation, immigration policy and asylum are a matter for inter-governmental co-operation. Citizens' rights are to be protected based on the standards of the Strasbourg European Court of Human Rights with provision for reporting and consultation with both the Commission and Parliament, although decision making is to be unanimous. The intention is to agree a common policy on political asylum. There will be police co-operation to combat drug trafficking and organised crime through Europol, the new police intelligence unit.

Among human rights organisations there is considerable concern about the consequences for civil liberties of the completion of the internal market as the focus shifts from controls at EC borders to intensified surveillance of target groups within the EC.

8.3 Key people

8.3.1 MEPs

Amédée Turner, Chair, Civil Liberties and International Affairs Committee

Ken Coates, Chair, Human Rights Subcommittee

Karel de Gucht (Liberal, Democratic and Reformist), Hoogstraat 9, 9290 Berlare, Belgium, Tel: 010 32 5 242 5386; Fax: 010 32 5 242 5388

8.3.2 In Britain

Liberty, 21 Tabard Street, London SE1 4LA, Tel: 071-403 3888

In addition, many of the contacts listed in sections 7.3 and 8.3 will be relevant to this section.

8.4 Funding

8.4.1 Humanitarian actions and defence of human rights

Over £3 million has been allocated exclusively for NGOs, with priority given to direct aid activities, both within the EC and in third countries. Suitable projects would include legal and medical assistance for torture victims, protecting political refugees and children, and raising the awareness of those in the legal profession and police forces. Grants vary from 1,000 to 250,000 ecu.

Further information from Daniela Napoli, Secretariat-General, EC Commission, Tel: 010 32 2 295 5501; Fax: 010 32 2 295 7850

8.4.2 Human rights and humanitarian affairs

The Secretariat-General of the Commission has set aside 2.8 million ecu for non-governmental organisations pursuing humanitarian aims and promoting human rights, for organisations of political refugees and for non-governmental organisations that carry out information work on the dangers of racism and fascism. Some of this is channelled through the European Human Rights Foundation (see ss 8.4.3). Topics covered include

- rehabilitation centres for torture victims and other projects giving practical assistance to victims of human rights violations;
- training officials who are called upon to ensure that human rights are respected (judges, lawyers, public officials, teachers, etc);
- strengthening respect for children's rights and helping children who are victims of human rights violations; and
- promoting training in organisations that promote human rights.

Priority is given to aid projects with a practical, direct impact. Research projects and academic seminars will be considered as funds allow.

Contact Mrs Daniela Napoli at the Commission's Brussels office, Tel: 010 32 2 295 5501; Fax: 010 32 2 295 7850 for an application form.

8.4.3 European Human Rights Foundation

Limited funds are available from the European Human Rights Foundation, established in 1980. Its objectives are the promotion and protection throughout the world of civil, political, economic, social and cultural rights, as they are at present laid down in the international instruments, as well as the furtherance of aims of a humanitarian nature in general. The foundation makes small grants, seldom exceeding 6,400 ecu (about £5,100) to individuals and/or non-governmental organisations for projects, and research in these fields, favouring small projects of an innovatory nature.

Recent examples include the funding of a summer camp for Arab and Jewish high school children, addressing controversial issues through co-operation; establishing an organisation to protect rights of children in Haiti; research on Muslim minorities in Europe; financial aid for human rights newsletter in Venezuela; setting up a grassroots human rights programme in India; establishing a legal aid project for victims of torture in Turkey; research into child labour in Asia and the publication of legal texts in Nepalese. Contact Peter Ashman, Director, European Human Rights Foundation, 13 rue Van Campenhout, 1040 Brussels, Tel: 010 32 2 734 9424; Fax: 010 32 2 734 6831.

8.4.4 Human rights and democracy in developing countries

There is a budget of nearly £13 million for 1993 to support initiatives in developing countries which aim to strengthen human rights and democracy by means of organising elections, giving logistical support to elected parliaments, strengthening judicial systems and supporting activities conducted by NGOs. Latin America is excluded from this budget, since it is covered by another. Contact Mr L Riera, Tel: 010 32 2 299 3243 or Mr Freiria, Tel: 010 32 2 295 2076, DG VIII, at the Commission, rue de la Loi 200, 1049 Brussels.

8.4.5 Support for democratisation in the Latin American region

This budget line has £12 million set aside for 1993 to support a range of initiatives such as the organisation of free elections and support for Latin American or European NGOs (of which the former are given a higher priority). Haiti and Cuba are given particular preference. Contact Mr Goldstein for Central America, Tel: 010 32 2 299 2290 or Mr Hernandez for South America, Tel: 010 32 2 295 3666, DG I, rue de la Loi 200, 1049 Brussels.

8.4.6 Aid for NGOs working to defend and promote human rights in Turkey

This new budget line in 1993 was allocated £400,000. Contact Mr Cendrowicz DG I at the Commission in Brussels: Tel: 010 32 2 299 0691.

8.4.7 Democratisation in ex-communist countries

Civil society in Poland

This programme aims to strengthen NGOs and social movements in Poland. It was set up in 1992 for a three-year period, with three basic components: (i) information and legal advice for NGOs; (ii) education and training programmes; and (iii) direct support for NGO projects.

Projects should be carried out mainly by Polish NGOs, who therefore have priority in applying for funding, but EC NGOs can take part by contributing their specialist knowledge in training and financing etc. Activities in partnership with EC NGOs will be encouraged. Contact should be made with the Co-operation Fund in Warsaw. The total budget is 3 million ecu. Further information from Mr Emilio Valli, DG/I/L/5, Tel: 010 32 2 295 2910, and the Co-operation Fund Warsaw: Ms M. Pleban, Tel: 010 48 2 693 5416; Fax: 010 48 2 692 5300.

Civil Society in the Czech Republic and in Slovakia

This programme strengthens NGOs and social movements in the Czech Republic and in Slovakia. Just as for Poland it has three basic components. The programme was approved in 1992. Only Czech and Slovak NGOs can apply for funding, but EC NGOs can take part by contributing their knowhow. Particular attention will be given to projects involving co-operation with an EC NGO. EC NGOs can also provide advice to the structure which will be responsible for supervising practical implementation. The total budget is 4 million ecu. Further information from Mr Fullenbach, DGL/L/5, at the Commission, rue de la Loi 200, 1049 Brussels, Tel: 010 32 2 299 2008.

Civil society in the former Soviet Union

A programme to contribute to the strengthening of civil society has been approved with a total budget of 1 million ecu. Contact Mr S O Mogensen, EC Commission, DGI/E/5, Tel: 010 32 2 295 6562.

8.5 Key publications

Europe and Poverty by Child Poverty Action Group, due late in 1993, £6.95 including p&p from CPAG, 1-5 Bath Street, London EC1V 9PY

The European Community and Human Rights, available from the Commission's information offices, 8 Storey's Gate, London SW1P 8AT, Tel: 071-973 1992; Fax: 071-973 1900

European Human Rights Foundation Annual Report 1992, from its London Office, 95A Chancery Lane, London WC2A 1DT, Tel: 071-405 6018/9

NGDO-EC News, published by the NGDO-EC Liaison committee, 62, Ave de Cortenberg, B-1040 Brussels

9 *Education and Culture*

This chapter is aimed at schools, universities and colleges, adult education institutes, local authorities, professional bodies, individual teachers, careers officers, researchers and students, cultural bodies and voluntary organisations which can claim an educational role in the broad sense or which are interested in the education of disadvantaged groups or in education generally. Trade unions should also be interested, particularly in the schemes to prepare children for working life (see Preparation for work with ss 9.4.1).

9.1 Key Commission department

Commissioner: Antonio Ruberti

Key official: Thomas O'Dwyer, director, task force for human resources, education, training and youth, Tel: 010 32 2 295 8535, Fax: 010 32 2 295 7295.

9.2 Extent of Community involvement

EC involvement in education has increased greatly with the 1992 and People's Europe initiatives. The COMETT programme encourages co-operation between universities, firms and research institutes. The ERASMUS programme enables students to spend some of their university training in another member state. LINGUA promotes foreign language teaching. The status of these programmes is reinforced in the Maastricht Treaty which includes a chapter on 'education, vocational training and youth'. This gives the objectives of EC education policy as

- to develop the European dimension in education, particularly through the teaching and dissemination of the languages of the member states;

- to encourage mobility of students and teachers, *inter alia* by encouraging the academic recognition of diplomas and periods of study;
- to promote co-operation between educational establishments;
- to develop exchanges of information and experience on issues common to the education systems of the member states;
- to encourage the development of youth exchanges and exchanges of socio-educational instructors; and
- to encourage the development of distance education.

Three of the objectives of vocational training are

- to facilitate access to vocational training and encourage mobility of instructors and trainees and particularly young people;
- to stimulate co-operation on training between educational or training establishments and firms; and
- to develop exchanges of information and experience on issues common to the training systems of the member states.

Vocational training and cultural work are relevant under the Treaty of Rome as areas of economic activity. EC interests in culture include freedom in cultural goods, enlarging the audience, including by promoting out-of-season tourism and conservation of the architectural heritage.

9.2.1 Legislation

EC nationals have the right of equal access to vocational and post-secondary training. Professional training is being harmonised in some sectors, such as medicine and midwifery, but since 1992 post-secondary qualifications obtained in one member state after at least three years' study have been recognised in all other member states, although a period of supervised practice or a test of competence may still be required. A second directive proposed under the People's Europe initiative would ensure general recognition of other vocational training and qualifications so that a period of practice in one member state would be recognised as proof of competence to practise in all member states. Legislation also provides for the equal admission of nationals from other member states to vocational training and apprenticeships. The Maastricht Treaty includes the right for citizens to move and reside freely in other member states. EC decisions concerning education policy are to be taken by co-decision (see ss 1.2.2).

The Broadcasting directive adopted in 1989 created a European-wide broadcasting area under a five-year programme (1991–5) with a grant of 200 million ecu.

9.2.2 Living abroad

Anyone wishing to live, work or study abroad should obtain form CVQE1 from their local employment offices. The Commission's free Citizens' Europe Advisory Service can be contacted between 2 and 5pm on Mondays on 071-973 1904. The Department of Trade and Industry Hotline, 081-200 1992, can be contacted for a copy of their booklet *Europe: Open for Professions*.

9.3 Key contacts

9.3.1 For guidance on funding and general information

Official bodies

Carole Bevis, Head of Management Services and Public Relations Department, Central Bureau for Educational Visits and Exchanges, Seymour Mews House, Seymour Mews, London W1H 9PE, Tel: 071-486 5101. The Central Bureau is the national office responsible for the provision of information and advice on all forms of educational visits and exchanges; the development and administration of a wide range of curriculum-related pre-service and in-service exchange programmes; the linking of education establishments and local education authorities with counterparts abroad; and the organisation of meetings and conferences related to professional international experience. The Bureau provides advice and information for local authorities, teachers and pupils, parents, non-student youth and others interested in educational visits and exchanges.

The British Council, Central Information Point, 10 Spring Gardens, London SW1A 2BN, Tel: 071-839 4382. The Council is another source on funding and on international links in general.

Voluntary organisations

The UK Centre for European Education (UKCEE), based in the Schools Unit of the Central Bureau (see under 'Official bodies' above). The UKCEE is one of 15 national centres all concerned with education about Europe in their own countries. These centres are linked together through an international secretariat. The UKCEE National Conference brings together all British organisations interested in a European dimension in primary, secondary, further and higher education. The UKCEE provides information through its twice yearly newsletter *EUROEDNEWS*, is involved in European activities and deals with curriculum development. It runs the European Curriculum Awards scheme in the UK.

Eva Evans, Secretary, University Association for Contemporary European Studies, King's College London, WC2R 2LS, Tel: 071-240 0206. UACES holds conferences and publishes registers of courses in European studies, research into European integration in the UK and conference proceedings.

In Brussels

EURYDICE (Education Information Network in the European Community) rue Archimède 17, 1040 Brussels. A joint venture between the Commission and the European Cultural Foundation, EURYDICE exchanges information on education between policy makers in the member states and EC institutions.

In Paris

European Institute of Education and Social Policy, Université de Paris, IX Dauphine, Place du Maréchal de Lattré de Tassigny 1, 75116 Paris, France, Tel: 010 33 1 4505 1410; Fax: 010 33 1 4553 8134. This institute is concerned with higher education and vocational and scientific training in Europe. It publishes the *European Journal of Education* and administers ERASMUS and EURYDICE in Brussels.

9.3.2 To lobby/for advice on lobbying

The Secretary of State for Education, Department of Education, Sanctuary Buildings, Great Smith Street, Westminster, London SW1P 3BT, Tel: 071-925 5000. The Secretary of State represents the UK at meetings of the Council of Education Ministers, and his officials are in constant touch with the Commission.

UK Euro-MPs

For members of the European Parliament Culture, Youth Education, and the Media Committee, consult the London office of the European Parliament, 2 Queen Anne's Gate, London SW1H 9AA, Tel: 071-222 0411; Fax: 071-222 2713.

Voluntary organisations

Graham Hitchin, British Youth Council, 57 Chalton Street, London NW1 1HU, Tel: 071-387 7559. The council is represented on the EC's Youth Forum, 120 rue Joseph II, 1040 Brussels, Tel: 010 32 2 230 6490. The Youth Forum lobbies the Commission, Parliament and Commission Institutions on education policies, youth exchanges, social issues and on third world development issues.

9.4 Funding – education

The Community provides funding for inter-EC co-operation, exchanges and mobility grants. Money available for education projects is dealt with in ss 9.4.1. Grants to individuals are covered in ss 9.4.3.

9.4.1 Grants for projects

General projects and research

Spreading information about the EC Work designed to promote awareness of, and spread information about, the European Community, may very occasionally be part-funded by the Commission's information budget. There is no formal scheme, but anybody with a good idea can try to interest the Commission in it. The target may be school children, young people or adults, so the scheme is not confined to those concerned with youth or with adult education.

There is no restriction on subject matter as long as it primarily relates to the EC. There is also flexibility regarding the means you choose to publicise. Seminars, courses and research (including surveys) for publication are the more obvious candidates for funding. You will stand a better chance of being funded if you choose a subject which shows the EC in a reasonable light, but you will not be expected to present anything other than a fair picture, including criticisms. Requests may be addressed to the Head of the London Office, 8 Storey's Gate, London SW1P 3AT.

Activities relevant to the EC The European Cultural Foundation's criteria for funding are also broad. The aim of this private, international body based in the Netherlands and established for over 30 years, is 'to promote cultural, scientific and educational activities of a multinational character and European inspiration'. Projects must seek to increase awareness of the European dimension of our societies. They should be concerned primarily either with basic values, culture, education, environment, international relations or with the problems of European society in general, excluding strictly scientific research. Projects should involve the collaboration of bodies from at least three, and preferably more, European countries. There is a preference for one of these to be outside the EC since the foundation covers the whole of western Europe. Funding is strictly on an annual basis.

Further information is available from James Took MBE, European Cultural Foundation (UK Committee), Pilgrims Appledore, nr Ashford, Kent TN26 2AE, Tel: 0233-83215 (the director's private number) or direct from the foundation's headquarters at 5 Jan van Goyenkade, 1075 HN Amsterdam, Tel: 010 31 20 76 0222; Fax: 010 31 20 75 2231. The UK Committee advises on applications from Britain but does not itself make the grants.

More specific areas of work

Education of immigrants Language and vocational training for migrant workers has been eligible for support from the Social Fund (see ss 3.4.1).

Education of the children of migrants   Studies and exchanges have covered the children of travellers and measures to combat illiteracy and skills problems for early school leavers. Further information from Education of the Children of Migrant Workers, EWH, Im Fort 7, 6740 Landau, Germany.

World development education   Funding is available for the education of any age group on the issues of world development (see ss 10.6.2).

Exchanges of experience between centres of adult education or training   The EC makes grants available towards the travel and subsistence of 'adult education' course organisers participating in cross-national workshops. The definition of adult education is a broad one, so conferences of community workers, social workers or local development agents, for example, would be eligible as would programmes for trainers and instructors. Those administering or initiating training may also apply.

The workshops must involve co-operation among, normally, at least three member states. They should cover social or vocational training for long-term unemployed adults or basic adult education, including literacy and numeracy, particularly involving the use of multi-media or distance education in local communities, or education and training measures linked to regional development programmes in disadvantaged areas – urban or rural. Further information is available from the Task Force at the Commission, rue de la Loi 200, 1049 Brussels.

Preparation for work   Article 128 of the Treaty of Rome commits the EC to 'lay down general principles for implementing a common vocational training policy capable of contributing to the harmonious development both of the national economies and the common market'. This is reinforced by the Maastricht Treaty and the Social Chapter. In December 1987, the Council adopted a Community programme to support the development and implementation of member states' policies for the vocational training of young people after the completion of their full-time compulsory education.

This European Community Action Programme, named PETRA, aims to prepare young people aged 16–27 for working life. Support is available for training or work experience placements in other member states for young people in initial vocational training below degree level, young workers, young job-seekers or those taking part in an advanced training programme (Action I). Support is also available within the European Network of Training Partnerships for the joint training of trainers and the development of European training modules (Action II). There is limited support for organisations who are concerned with adding a European dimension to vocational information and guidance (Action III). Over 240 cross-border training projects are already in operation, with a total budget of 15 million ecu (over £10 million) in 1991.

For information on Actions I and II contact: Jane Owen, Central Bureau for Educational Visits and Exchanges, Seymour Mews House, Seymour Mews, London W1H 9PE, Tel: 071-486 5101; Fax: 071-935 5741.
For information on Action III and general measures contact: David Oatley, Department of Employment, European Training, Room 513, Steel House, Tothill Street, London SW1H 9NF, Tel: 071-273 5660; Fax: 071-273 5475.
The Brussels contact is Ifaplan, Square Ambiorix 32, 1040 Brussels.

Youth exchanges In May 1988, the Council adopted a programme called 'Youth for Europe' which provides funding for multinational projects with jointly conducted activities which have a social or cultural focus. The exchanges can last for 7 days in Western Europe, 10 days in Eastern Europe or 21 days elsewhere in the world. They must involve young people aged 15–25. Funds are provided to cover the travel costs of the visitors and the costs incurred by the hosts, and national organisers should ensure a match between the levels of expenditure in each country. Political projects, performance tours, competitive sports tours, tourist visits and one-way visits do not qualify for support. The programme had a budget of 6.5 million ecu (£4.5 million) in 1991.
Further information is available from Jeunesse pour l'Europe, Place du Luxembourg 2–3, 1040 Brussels; or the Youth Exchange Centre within the British Council (see ss 9.3.1).

International non-governmental youth organisation There is limited support (about £580,000 in 1993) to finance an annual programme of activities for non-governmental youth organisations with affiliated organisations in several member states. Attention is paid to the Community aspects and quality of the programmes. Applications to cover support for a single budget year should arrive by 30 April of the relevant year.
Further information is available from Mr Bourges-Maunoury, Division C1, Secretariat General, EC Commission, Brussels, Tel: 010 32 2 295 2160/6480.

Go and See Grants The Prince's Trust provides 150 grants of up to £500 for contact between young people making links with others in the same field from different member states. Contact Anne Engel, The Prince's Trust, 8 Bedford Row, London WC1R 4BA, Tel: 071-430 0524; Fax: 071-831 7280.

9.4.2 Grants to institutes

Co-operation in higher education

Under ERASMUS, the European Community Action Scheme for the

Mobility of University Students, support is available for colleges organising short, intensive courses involving students from several member states or exchange programmes with other EC colleges (see 9.4.2, University students and teachers). Grants are also payable to groups of universities acting on a European basis to make new initiatives in specific fields better known throughout the Community. Publications which increase awareness of study and teaching opportunities in other member states and of inter-college co-operation throughout the EC also come under the ERASMUS programme, as does the development of a course credit transfer system. Finance for 1992–3 was 100 million ecu (approximately £80 million), which included support for the LINGUA programme and for the participation of EFTA countries.

Further information is available from the UK ERASMUS, Students Grants Council, The University, Canterbury CT3 7PD, Tel: 0227-762712; or from ERASMUS Bureau, 70 rue de Montoyer, 1040 Brussels, Tel: 010 32 2 233 0111; Fax: 010 32 2 233 0150.

Aid to institutes training scientific and technical managers from developing countries

The EC has funds which enable it to support and guide the activities of European, or in some cases, third world institutes providing training for scientific and technical students from the developing countries. Projects may be co-financed or fully funded. Further information is available from Mr B Amat Armengol or Mm M Neves (DG VIII) at the Commission, rue de la Loi 200, 1049 Brussels, Tel: 010 32 2 299 3212 or 010 32 2 299 2538.

LINGUA

The LINGUA programme is designed to strengthen the teaching of other EC languages – for the UK: Danish, Dutch, French, German, Greek, Irish, Italian, Luxembourgish, Portuguese and Spanish. It promotes the in-service training of foreign language teachers, inter-university co-operation programmes, student mobility and mobility and exchange of teaching staff in co-operation with ERASMUS; the development of teaching materials and self-learning methods to increase knowledge of foreign languages used in work relations and economic life; exchanges for young people undergoing professional, vocational and technical education within the Community where a European language is included, and supporting activities such as back-up European associations and dissemination of the results of LINGUA; and foreign language materials for general use particularly in the least widely taught languages. The budget for 1990–4 is 200 million ecu (£160 million).

Further information is available from Rosemary Martin, UK LINGUA Office, Seymour Mews House, Seymour Mews, London W1H 9PE, Tel:

071-725 9493; Fax: 071-224 1906; or Bureau Lingua, 10 rue du Commerce, 1040 Brussels.

Joint training projects, courses and multi-media training systems in the field of new technology/university/enterprise co-operation

Part-funding is available from the COMETT (Co-operation between Universities and Enterprises on Training in the Field of Technology) programme for work devising, developing and testing at European level projects for ongoing training. The second phase of the COMETT project (1990–4) also includes the European Free Trade Association (EFTA) countries: Austria, Finland, Iceland, Liechtenstein, Norway, Sweden and Switzerland. It hopes to place 25,000 students from firms in other member states.

There must be co-operation between business and universities or colleges. Support is available for ongoing courses ensuring that the results of research and development in new technology are passed on rapidly in universities and businesses. Multi-media systems developed cross-nationally and using new information and communication technologies are also eligible. COMETT projects need to take particular account of the training needs of small and medium-sized businesses.

Funding is also available under COMETT for university-enterprise training partnerships to co-operate in a European network. One of your objectives must be transnational co-operation, particularly to organise training schemes to exchange staff, trainees or training officers or to develop joint training materials. Preference will be given to schemes involving several universities and businesses, co-operating either on a regional basis or by subject.

The COMETT guide for applicants is available from the UK COMETT Liaison Office, Department of Education, Sanctuary Buildings, Great Smith Street, London SW1P 3BT. Contact Miss Moss (071-925 5306) for the European network of university-enterprise training partnerships and cross-border exchanges, and Mr Comport (Tel: 071-925 5254; Fax: 071-925 5379) for projects to promote continuing training in the technology sector and multi-media distance education. COMETT's budget is 230 million ecu for 1990–4 for all member states.

TEMPUS

The Trans-European Mobility Scheme was launched in April 1992 for the benefit of central and eastern European countries. It aids youth exchanges and the mobility of students in higher education with the aim of promoting the development of education and training systems. There are three main schemes: support for joint training projects, mobility aid for teachers, trainers and students, and aid for complementary activities. It has so far been used by some 10,500 members of staff and 6,400 students. Only 15 per cent of applications, on average, are successful. Finance for 1993–4 is about 107 million ecu (£82 million). The Commission is proposing the extension of the programme to 1998 and to the republics of the former USSR. Further information available from Europe Unit, Education and Science Division, The British Council, 10 Spring Gardens, London SW1A 2BN, Tel: 071-957 7076; Fax: 071-957 7561.

Cheap Food

Surplus EC foods are sometimes made available to non-profit-making organisations (see ss 4.4.5).

Research and development

The EC funds cross border research co-operation by businesses, universities and public and private research institutes. Areas covered include environment (see ss 11.5.8), marine sciences, biotechnology (see ss 11.5.15), agriculture, biomedics and health (see ss 12.4.2) and human capital and mobility. For more information, see *EC Research Funding*.

9.4.3 Grants to individuals

Trainees and trainers

The COMETT programme described above provides grants for trainees, including new graduates, being trained in undertakings in another member state, fellowships for university staff seconded to undertakings in other member states and fellowships for business personnel seconded to universities in other member states.

University students and teachers

The ERASMUS programme provides for the establishment and operation of a European university network designed to promote inter-university teacher exchanges as well as a student exchange programme so that students can spend a period of study in another member state as part of their overall course. Full grants and partial grants to cover the extra costs of studying abroad have so far been awarded to a total of 150,000 students and the Maastricht Treaty implies increasing the numbers for the future. Grants are only awarded where the period of study will gain full recognition by the student's home college. They cover at least one term, but are not normally awarded for the first year of university/college study.

Students may apply on an individual basis to the national grant-awarding authorities or through an inter-university co-operation programme, but priority is given to applications which form part of a programme. For the academic year 1993-4, a total of 99,000 applications for the ERASMUS scheme were received, of which 20,000 were from UK students. Applications must be sent to the ERASMUS bureau at least six months before the visit is due to take place. UK ERASMUS, Students Grants Council, The University, Canterbury CT3 7PD, Tel: 0227-762712; or ERASMUS Bureau, 70 due de Montoyer, 1040 Brussels, Tel: 010 32 2 233 0111; Fax: 010 32 2 233 0150.

Schoolchildren

Only the children of coal-miners and steel-workers killed by an occupational disease or accident are eligible for help with schooling and with training from the EC. To apply for what is called a Paul Finet Scholarship, contact the Coal Industry Social Welfare Organisation, 27 Huddersfield Road, Barnsley S70 2LX, Tel: 0226-298871; the Iron and Steel Trades Confederation, Swinton House, 324 Gray's Inn Road, London WC1X 8DD, tel: 071-837 6691; or the Secretary General, Paul Finet Foundation, JMO/C4/26A, Jean Monnet Building, plateau du Kirchberg, Luxembourg.

Scientists and engineers

The European Commission encourages the mobility and training of young scientists and engineers at various stages of training by awarding contracts which cover grants and courses. The young scientists participate in Community research concerned with energy, the environment and reference materials and methods. Those eligible are students completing university studies and preparing a thesis, young research workers preparing a doctorate or scientists with a doctorate or at least five years' experience of research. Grants cover a maximum of one year, three years or two years respectively. Applicants should send details of their subject area to the European Commission, Scientific and Technical Information (DC XII) at the Commission, rue de la Loi 200, 1049 Brussels. Further information is available from Mr Pozzo (Italian), Tel: 010 32 2 299 1111.

Students from the African, Caribbean and Pacific (ACP) countries

The Lomé Convention (see s 10.5) provides for EC awards for the training of ACP citizens either in their home country or in member states of the Community. Applicants must be nominated by their own government, which submits proposals to the local delegation of the European Commission. Further information is available from Directorate-General VIII at the Commission, rue de la Loi 200, 1049 Brussels.

Three months' study at the European Parliament

Robert Schumann scholarship holders spend up to three months at the Secretariat of the European Parliament with the Directorate for Research and Documentation, and are expected to complete one or more study projects. For further information contact that Directorate-General at the European Parliament, Bâtiment Robert Schumann, Plateau du Kirchberg, Luxembourg; or from the European Parliament, 2 Queen Anne's Gate, London, SW1H 9AA, Tel: 071-222 0411.

Training as stagiaires

Training of five months within the Commission is offered to young graduates to help them find out how the Community works. For further information contact the Bureau de Stages at the Commission, rue de la Loi 200, 1049 Brussels.

Research into European integration

Twenty research grants are open in some years to young (under age 40) university teachers at the start of their career, who, individually or as a team, are doing research work on European integration. For further information and application forms write to University information at the Commission, rue de la Loi 200, 1049 Brussels.

Jean Monnet Fellowships

Thirty of these are offered annually to academics wishing to spend a year in full-time research at the European University Institute in Florence. Application forms can be obtained from the Academic Service, European University Institute, CP No 2355, 50100 Firenze, Ferrovia (FI), Italy.

Jean Monnet Project

Funding is available for the co-financing of new, three-year teaching posts which would enable the development of European Studies courses and academic research into European integration. Financial support was given to 45 new European chairs in 1992, so that the total number of full-time teaching posts entirely devoted to European integration is now 135. A *vade mecum* and application forms can be obtained by writing to University Information: Jean Monnet Project, DG X, the Commission, rue de la Loi 200, 1049 Brussels.

Under 36-year-olds writing on Europe

The Irene Scizier prize is awarded annually for a single work, a series of articles or studies already published, or the complete works of a candidate, on the Common Agricultural Policy or dealing with the dissemination of information on agriculture or with policy for the dissemination of information about Community affairs in general. Apply for further information to the Irene Scizier prize at the Commission, rue de la Loi 200, 1049 Brussels. The annual deadline for submissions is mid March.

Emile Nöel Prize

The prize, created in 1981 with the co-operation of European Community officials, is awarded annually to mark an exemplary action or initiative designed to inspire public opinion and particularly young people, with renewed enthusiasm for furthering the European idea. Further information is available from Mr Jean Danis, 13 rue R Follereau, L-8027 Strassen, Luxembourg, Tel: 010 352 310050.

Administrators, teachers and post-graduate researchers in higher education and careers staff

The EC's 'short study visit scheme' supplies grants to individuals for up to four weeks' study of educational systems in other member states (preferably more than one). For further information contact the Task Force at the Commission, rue de la Loi 200, 1049 Brussels.

Short study visits for education specialists

The ARION Programme, the European Community Programme of short study visits for local and regional educationists, provides travel expenses and subsistence allowances for one-week visits to examine specific aspects of educational provision in another European Community country. The scheme, covering a given range of themes, is open to local education authority administrators, advisers, head teachers, teacher trainers and inspectors on the nomination of their chief officer.

Themes for 1993–4 include a general study of primary and secondary education, information technology in education, the integration of special needs pupils into mainstream education, failure at school, the European dimension and teacher training.

Further information is available from the ARION Programme Assistance Unit, Padagogischer Austauschdienst, Nassestrasse 8, 5300 Bonn 1, Germany, or from the Central Bureau for Educational Visits and Exchanges.

A study scheme for training specialists started in 1985 to enable visits to training centres in other Community countries. It is organised by CEDEFOP (see ss 3.4.7) and in the UK by the Employment Department. Those responsible for training or training specialists who can be expected to disseminate the information gained and make use of their findings are eligible. The visits cover five working days, which are used to study aspects of other member states' systems, in particular the training of young people and adults and the application of technology. A number of places each year will be filled by people involved to some degree with EC action programmes, FORCE, PETRA and EUROTECNET. Applicants should contact Karen Newnham, Room N704, European Training, Moorfoot, Sheffield S1 4PQ, Tel: 0742-594359.

LINGUA

Grants are available to foreign language teachers, teacher trainers and those organising in-service training activities in another member state under the LINGUA programme. UK LINGUA office, Seymour Mews House, Seymour Mews, London W1H 9PE, Tel: 071-725 9493; Fax: 071-224 1906; or Bureau Lingua, 10 rue du Commerce, 1040 Brussels.

9.5 Culture

9.5.1 Extent of Community involvement

Under Article 36 of the EC Treaty the Community is concerned with 'national treasures possessing artistic, historic or archaeological value' and procedures to protect them. The Maastricht Treaty confirms EC commitment to increase cultural awareness, to encourage the conservation of buildings which have a wider European interest, and to develop the audio-visual sector. The Community will contribute to the improvement of the knowledge of the culture and history of the European peoples, not only through conservation measures but also through non-commercial cultural exchanges. It is also interested in the audio-visual arts and in the promotion of artistic creation generally, including through business sponsorship. A European Committee for Business, the Arts and Culture is being set up with its base in London. The completion of the internal market implies an EC interest in the free movement of cultural goods and services, author's rights and cross-border television.

9.5.2 Funding

Grants are available for cultural activities such as restoration of historic monuments, conserving and promoting architectural heritage and cultural exchanges. There may be opportunities for training and mobility scholarships in art restoration.

Preserving Europe's cultural heritage

Proposals are due on preserving and exploiting cultural riches both past and present and developing their potential as tourist attractions (museums, galleries and libraries), whether by means of records, videos or films.

Conserving and promoting the Community's architectural heritage

The Commission has supported work in this field for the last ten years. All projects submitted for funding must correspond with the year's theme. In 1991 the Community theme was 'Testimonies to human activities in industry and agriculture and crafts', in 1992 'Integrated upgrading of public spaces in historic centres', and in 1993 'Historical gardens and green spaces'. Community support of up to £100,000 may be given to cover up to 25 per cent of the conservation costs of such projects. Details and application forms may be obtained from the Cultural Action division of the Commission, Brussels address, from its information offices in London, Belfast, Cardiff and Edinburgh, or from English Heritage Historic Buildings and Monuments Commission for England, Fortress House, 23–25 Savile Row, London W1X 2HE; Historic Buildings and Monuments, Scottish Development Department, 20 Brandon Street, Edinburgh EH3 5RA; CADW Welsh Historic Monuments, Brunel House, 2 Fitzalan Road, Cardiff CF2 1UY; and Historic Monuments and Buildings Branch, 5–33 Hill Street, Belfast BT1 1LA. The Commission also funds work under its environmental action programme to combat the effects of atmospheric pollution on historic monuments.

European Community liberary prizes

An annual prize is awarded for a contribution to contemporary European literature. The submission may be in any literary genre such as novels, short stories, drama, essays or poetry. They must be written in one of the official languages (including Irish). The prize is 20,000 ecu (£16,000). In addition to this up to 25,000 ecu (£20,000) may be granted to translate the prize-winning work into the other languages of the Community. Each member state nominates up to three separate works for consideration by the European jury. Apply as for 'Translations of contemporary literary works' below.

European Community translation prize

An annual prize will be awarded to a translator for an outstanding translation of a significant work of contemporary European literature of any literary genre. The translation must be written in one of the official languages (including Irish). The prize is 20,000 ecu (£16,000). Each member state nominates up to three separate translations for consideration by the European jury. Apply as for 'Translations of contemporary literary works' below.

Translations of contemporary literary works

Grants are available for translating contemporary literary works, meaning literature published for the first time in the twentieth century – with preference given to those first published after 1945. This may include works whose publication in the European market is not considered viable without a Community grant. Priority will be given to works written in or being translated into one of the Community's minority languages. In 1991 76 projects were selected. Bursaries have been given to five European colleges of literary translation, with a budget of 140,000 ecu distributed among them. Application forms are available from Dr Alastair Niven, Director of Literature, Arts Council of Great Britain, 14 Great Peter Street, London SW1P 3NQ or from the Commission's Cultural Activities Division Office JECL 2/116, rue de la Loi 200, 1049 Brussels.

Script Development Fund

An annual sum of £1.5 million is now provided by the EC television and film institutions to encourage script writing in the independent film and television sector. All kinds of fiction projects except cartoons are eligible. Applications from teams of writers–producers or writers–directors have priority over those coming from writers alone. Successful applications will be 'of high quality, of interest to at least two member states, and likely to be produced'. Assuming production takes place, the grant is repayable on the first day of principal photography. Further information is available from the Script Fund Office at the British Film Institute, 21 Stephen Street, London W1P 1PL, Tel: 071-255 1444.

The EC has funded a number of projects under Media 92, a scheme to promote awareness of the importance of a strong audio-visual industry, which reflects the European identity and is able to compete with overseas industries. The aim was increased mobility of personnel and goods connected with the industry and better co-operation within Europe on the financing, production and distribution of audio-visual programmes, as well as a closer partnership between cinema and television.

Kaleidoscope

This is an award scheme by which the Commission provides up to 30,000 ecu or 25 per cent of total costs to a wide spectrum of cultural and artistic events. To be eligible the entries must seek to highlight European cultural traditions or stimulate co-operation and dialogue in relation to cultural activities. They must also involve at least three member states and be primarily non-profit making. Entry forms may be obtained from the London office of the EC, 8 Storey's Gate, London SW1P 3AT, Tel: 071-973 1992. They are normally issued in the early autumn and must be returned within a month or two for projects which take place in the following year.

Cultural projects involving people with disabilities

The EC, through the NGO EUCREA, supports innovative cultural projects involving people with disabilities from at least four EC member states. Application for grants of around £5,000 should go in the first place to the National Disability Arts Forum by the end of September in one year for funding in the next. Contact Katherine Walsh, National Disability Arts Forum, 28 Coombes Lane, Northfield, Birmingham B31 4QW.

9.6 Sport

The Commission contributes towards the cost of occasional sporting events as part of the EC's efforts to bring the Community closer to the people. For example, it aided the first European Community Club Team Swimming Championships staged at Leeds in April 1987, and has continued to support the games annually since then. The sporting events should be national or intentional events recognised by the national or international federations concerned. The organisers need to have expertise and experience.

The purpose of EC funding is to add a European dimension to the competition, and substantial media coverage should be expected. The Commission will not fund events which are associated with the names of alcohol or tobacco products. Grants can range from £1,000 to £200,000. In 1992, almost £1 million, one-fifth of the EC's budget set aside to strengthen EC citizens' feelings of belonging to the Community, went to sports events.

Further information from Gian Pietro Fontana-Rava, DG X, Audio-Visual, Information, Communication and Culture, at the Commission's Brussels address, Tel: 010 32 2 299 9366; Fax: 010 32 2 299 9284.

9.7 Key publications

The EC has established 44 European Documentation Centres in major UK university libraries. These exist primarily to provide access to information about the EC for students and academic institutions. A list of these centres is available from the EC's information offices.

Brussels in focus, EC access for sport, by Bill Seary, Sports Council, 1992 £10

A Career in the Commission of the European Communities, available from 8 Storey's Gate, London SW1P 3AT, Tel: 071-973 1992; Fax: 071-973 1900

EC Research Funding, EC Commission, available from 8 Storey's Gate, London SW1P 3AT, Tel: 071-973 1992; Fax: 071-973 1900

Education and Training, available free from 8 Storey's Gate, London SW1P 3AT, Tel: 071-973 1992; Fax: 071-973 1900

Education and Training Programmes, background report, 14 December 1992, EC London office, 8 Storey's Gate, London SW1P 3AT, Tel: 071-973 1992; Fax: 071-973 1900

ERASMUS News, available from HMSO or the ERASMUS Bureau, 15 rue d'Arlon, 1040 Brussels, Tel: 010 32 2 233 0111

EUROEDNEWS, a newsletter, produced twice a year by the UK Centre for European Education, Schools Unit, Central Bureau for Educational Visits and Exchanges, Seymour Mews House, Seymour Mews, London W1H 9DE, Tel: 071-486 5101

The European Community and Sport, EC Commission, available free from 8 Storey's Gate, London SW1P 3AT, Tel: 071-973 1992; Fax: 071-973 1900

The European Community Audiovisual Policy, EC Commission, available free from 8 Storey's Gate, London SW1P 3AT, Tel: 071-973 1992; Fax: 071-973 1900

Comparability of vocational training qualifications, from Task Force Human Resources, Vocational Training Unit, rue de la Loi 200, 1049 Brussels

The European Teacher, annual journal of the UK section of the European Association of Teachers, free to members

The European Journal of Education, published by the European Institute of Education and Social Policy, Université de Paris, IX Dauphine, Place du Marchèl de Lattre de Tassigny, 75116 Paris, Tel: 010 33 1 4505 1410; Fax: 010 33 1 4553 8134

Freedom of Movement, available free from 8 Storey's Gate, London SW1P 3AT, Tel: 071-973 1992; Fax: 071-973 1900

Guide to Sources of Funding for Educational Visits and Exchanges, available from Policy Research and European Affairs Unit of Mid-Glamorgan County Council, County Council Offices, Greyfriars Road, Cardiff CF1 3LG, Tel: 0222-820069, Fax: 0222-820829

The Impact of European Community Policies for Research and Technological Development upon Science and Technology in the United Kingdom, published by HMSO

Science and Technology in Europe, available free from 8 Storey's Gate, London SW1P 3AT, Tel: 071-973 1992; Fax: 071-973 1900

A Young People's Europe, available free from 8 Storey's Gate, London SW1P 3AT, Tel: 071-973 1992; Fax: 071-973 1900

10 The Outside World

This chapter is of particular interest to non-governmental bodies with aid projects in developing countries, eastern Europe and the former Soviet Union, including schemes concerned with human rights, aids, drugs and ecology. World development is the only field of EC interest where a prominent place has been given to the work of voluntary organisations, with a special budget allocation for co-funding their projects, specialised Commission staff and a well-developed network of communication (see s 10.3). Development NGOs and other movements which have specialised in development issues are eligible for the EC's budget allocation for education of the European public on development issues.

10.1 Key Commission department

Development: Directorate-General VIII

Commissioner: Manuel Marin (Spanish)

Acting Director-General: Peter Pooley (British) Tel: 010 32 2 299 3238

Key officials: Bernard Ryelandt (Belgian), responsible for co-operation with NGOs, Tel: 010 32 2 299 9861; Carola Koester (German), deals with British NGOs, Tel: 010 32 2 299 3004; Karen Birchall (British), deals with development education, Tel: 010 32 2 299 2972; Fax: 010 32 2 299 2847; Anton Reithinger (German), deals with food aid, Tel: 010 32 2 299 9857; Fax: 010 32 2 299 3073; Gomez Reino, ECHO, deals with non-food emergency aid, Tel: 010 32 2 295 4249; Fax: 010 32 2 299 2876.
PHARE, central and eastern Europe, S. Christiane/M. Grell, DG 1/L/5, Tel: 010 32 2 1900/1980.
CIS, S Mogensen, DG1/E/5, Tel: 010 32 2 295 6562.

10.2 Extent of Community involvement

The European Community has exclusive control over trade policy with the rest of the world, including the developing countries. It also has its own aid budget, the European Development Fund, amounting with other EC aid to about the same size as the official UK aid budget. The Maastricht Treaty contains a chapter confirming the EC commitment to providing aid to developing countries and to multi-annual programmes. Over the last three years, the EC has also been trying to help the countries of central and eastern Europe to establish a market economy, stimulate private initiative, exchange information and contacts and strengthen their competitiveness.

10.3 EC-NGDO Network

NGOs interested in EC development policies and aid are represented in an annual assembly, with an elected Liaison Committee which advises the Commission of NGO views on EC policies on developing countries and the co-funding of voluntary organisations' projects. The Community now funds a small secretariat for the Committee.

The member organisations from each member state meet together in Brussels each spring. Once every three years each 'national meeting' elects a representative on to the Liaison Committee. The British representative up to April 1995 is Julian Filochowski of the Catholic Fund for Overseas Development (CAFOD). The 12 national representatives are joined on the Liaison Committee by the three presidents of the Committee's working groups, which are also constituted from nationally elected representatives.

Over 70 British organisations, which have dealings with the EC on development issues, are currently represented through the UK EC-NGDO Network. The Commission prefers NGOs to be members of their national networks before entering into co-financing arrangements with them. Although the UK EC-NGDO Network does not deal with individual requests for co-financing of projects, which go straight to the Commission, it is an important channel of influence. It has succeeded, for example, in getting the budget allocation for NGOs raised substantially.

If your organisation wants to join the UK EC-NGDO Network you should contact Julian Filochowski at the address given under ss 10.4.1. If eligible for membership you can expect to attend two assemblies, in spring and autumn, as well as to receive invitations to attend specialist working parties.

10.4 Key people

10.4.1 In Britain

Julian Filochowski, British representative on the NGO Liaison Committee. Address: EC–NGO Network, c/o CAFOD, 2 Romero Close, Stockwell Road, London SW9 9TY, Tel: 071-733 7900.

10.4.2 In Brussels

James Mackie, Liaison Committee of Development NGOs to the European Communities, Square Ambiorix 10, 1040 Brussels, Tel: 010 32 2 736 4087; Fax: 010 32 2 732 1934.

Simon Stocker, Eurostep, rue Stévin 115, 1040 Brussels, Tel: 010 32 2 231 1659; Fax: 010 32 2 230 3780.

Peter Crossman, European Ecumenical Organisation for Development, 1040 Brussels, Tel: 010 32 2 230 6105. This is a lobbying organisation which represents the churches of the EC. For the addresses of other church organisations in Brussels, see ss 4.3.2.

10.5 Current EC policies and campaigning issues

The centrepiece of the EC's development policy is the Lomé Convention, which offers over 70 developing countries in Africa, the Caribbean and the Pacific aid and trade preferences over other non-member states. Lomé is regularly renegotiated. The fourth convention began on 1 March 1990 and will remain in force for 10 years.

ACP countries receive their aid from the European Development Fund, as well as concessions such as Stabex, a form of insurance policy for developing countries reliant upon a limited number of cash crops. Stabex is intended to provide compensation when falling prices lead to substantial shortfalls in income. Other developing countries, mainly in Asia and Latin America, receive aid from the EC's own budget and some trade concessions under the Generalised System of Preferences.

British voluntary organisations have criticised the dumping of EC agricultural surpluses, especially sugar and beef, on the world market, and EC restrictions on imports from developing countries, such as those imposed under the Multi-fibre Arrangement. They want to see EC policies favour the poorest countries, not only the ACP. They have welcomed the gradual trend in EC policies away from routine food aid and towards national development strategies aimed at stimulating local agriculture.

10.6 Developing countries

This is one field where substantial, though still insufficient, funds are made available specifically to voluntary organisations. A special allocation within the Commission's budget usually contributes up to 50 per cent towards NGOs' projects in developing countries and, at home, on development education. Very occasionally, 75 per cent financing is granted. The larger voluntary organisations may act as a channel for emergency and food aid, and a number of newer funds, some with an environmental slant, have been established.

The EC's financial year runs with the calendar year so the best time to apply for funding from the smaller budget lines is late in one year for funding in the next. It is best to apply between October and the end of March for co-financing. Funds for a specific calendar year have usually been fully allocated by October in that year. Co-financed long-term development projects typically take 6–9 months from application to contract with a further wait of 6–8 weeks for the arrival of funds.

10.6.1 Co-financing of work in the developing countries

Key document: *General Conditions for the Co-financing of Projects Undertaken in Developing Countries by Non-governmental Organisations*, available from the Commission. Obtain the current edition to check the details.

Key contact: The person who deals with applications from British NGOs is Carola Koester, Tel: 010 32 2 299 3004.

Requirements of your organisation

Co-financing of schemes for development in developing countries is open to any non-profit making NGO, firmly based in Britain or another member state, which is able to assure the Commission of its soundness in financial and organisational matters. Account will be taken of the amount of private support your organisation is able to attract, the priority it gives to overseas development activities, its previous experience, including that of co-financing, either with the Commission or with the British government, and the nature and extent of its links with local counterparts in the developing countries and within the EC.

Current requirements of your project

The initiative for your project should come from its beneficiaries. A primary aim of the programme is to increase the local partners' confidence in self-development, so the beneficiaries should be involved as partners in all stages of a project's planning, implementation and, on completion, management.

The local partners should be clearly identifiable. Increasing account is being taken of the effect on, and involvement of, local women.

The projects must be sound economically, financially, technically, sociologically and culturally. You should therefore demonstrate that your project is likely to continue after external aid has ceased. You must have clearly defined objectives, obtainable within a specified timetable. Your project must be compatible with the development objectives of the recipient country and, in principle, must have been accepted by the appropriate authorities in the country concerned (though not necessarily at a national level).

Other guidelines

Your project will stand a better chance of acceptance if it is development rather than welfare or relief orientated. It is also an advantage if funds are generated which can be re-used for other projects. Officials will be looking for training/educational content and for projects which promote the economic and social progress of the most deprived sections of the population. In 1982 preference began to be given to projects increasing food production, and the Commission has praised the work of voluntary organisations on small-scale agricultural projects, producing food for local consumption. These are likely to remain high on the priority list.

Other areas of work encouraged under the current programme are social infrastructure, preventive medicine, vocational training and human development. Projects solely concerned with formal education, curative medicine and basic research, as well as seminars, study trips, etc receive lower priority. The main sectors covered have been rural development, training and health. Others dealt with have been production, migrants and refugees, and communications.

Geographic guidelines

From the Commission's point of view, the purpose of co-financing is for voluntary bodies to help spend EC money in the less developed countries in areas where the Commission and member states would find it difficult to reach the poorest sections of the community. Preference is therefore given to projects in largely rural areas, regions and countries with weak infrastructures and/or those without governmental projects. Projects in any of the developing countries, as defined by the United Nations, are eligible. There is no preference for signatory countries of the Lomé Convention; if anything the Commission is seeking to counterbalance the previous emphasis on Lomé countries in this programme.

Scale of funding

The EC normally pays up to 50 per cent of costs. The current ceiling is about £120,000 per year with a maximum of £360,000 over three years or £400,000 over five years. The minimum request considered is about £9,600. The Commission's definition of the costs of a project is comprehensive. It includes salaries for people directly and substantially involved in implementing the project on the spot, administrative costs at home (up to 6 per cent), development education work within the EC on that project and the value of 'in kind' contributions such as labour where these are clearly documented.

At least 15 per cent of the funding should come from the voluntary organisation's funds rather than all from central government. If the project justifies it, it may pay to think big and put in a substantial request for funds, since it will be less time-consuming for the Commission than separate applications for many small projects. Similarly, a 'consortium approach' – making a claim together with other NGOs working in the same area or field – may help and can sometimes double the Commission's maximum contribution.

Block grants

When co-financing with the Commission has been satisfactory for three out of the last five years, your organisation will become eligible to receive a lump sum for several projects. The Commission will contact you directly if this is the case.

How to apply

The details of applying, as well as the official conditions for co-financing, are contained in *General Conditions for the Co-financing of Projects Undertaken in Developing Countries by Non-governmental Organisations*. These conditions will form part of the contract if you are successful in your bid for funding, so study them carefully. At the same time as you apply for this document, you will find it useful to contact the national representative to the NGDO Committee, so that you can be added to the EC–NGDO network mailing list (see s 10.3).

If you are considering requesting funding from the Commission for the first time, get advice before making a formal application. The Commission officials are frank and friendly. They will advise you on whether your project is eligible for funds and how your application could be improved. Start by writing a preliminary letter, outlining what you want to do and what your organisation's functions are. Explain how you fit into the EC and UK development network. Who set you up? Are you church-based, for example? Do you concentrate on any particular field of activity (such as health)? Do you have any links with organisations in the rest of the EC? Mention any previous experience of working with government money and that you are in touch with the Liaison Committee. If you discover that your application stands a chance of success, you may need to visit the Commission to discuss your project and your organisation's credentials.

Once you have worked with the Commission, you will not need to visit Brussels to support every application. Your documents will simply be passed to the technical and geographic divisions for a decision based on the guidelines given in *General conditions* and influenced by the latest Commission thinking. It should normally be sufficient to stay in touch by telephone.

10.6.2 Co-financing projects at home – in development education

Key document: *General Conditions for the Co-financing of Projects to Raise Public Awareness of Development Issues, Carried Out by Non-governmental Organisations in the European Community.* Obtain the most up-to-date version from Karen Birchall, DG VIII, at the Commission's Brussels address.

Following a request from the NGOs, about 10 per cent of the co-financing budget has been set aside for educating the public at home on development issues. This is slightly more over-subscribed than the co-financing of developing country projects. The NGDO–EC Liaison Committee has a development education working group.

European networks, working with this group, currently cover industrial restructuring, agricultural restructuring, film making, formal education (schools), women in development, cultures and development South and North, and towns and development.

Eligible organisations

As with the co-financing of developing country projects, your organisation must be non-profit making, firmly based in a member state and able to assure the Commission of its soundness in financial and organisational matters.

Eligible projects

Projects should be aimed at influencing opinion on subjects concerning relations between Europe and developing countries and the influence of each upon the other, or should be national projects which can be shown to have relevance to EC policies and their impact on developing countries, or which propose joint projects with organisations elsewhere in the EC. They should encourage solidarity with developing countries and public awareness of Europe's interdependence with developing countries. Projects that have been funded in the past have set up courses for schools, churches and workers, co-ordinated work at EC level, produced audiovisual materials, and conducted seminars and campaigns. One campaign, for example, aimed to make farmers aware of the relationship between EC agricultural production and food problems in the developing countries. Another project produced a permanent information programme on extreme poverty in the world.

If you are to be successful in obtaining funding, you also need to show that you are very clear about what you want to achieve and whom you are trying to influence.

Scale of funding

The EC pays up to half the cost of the project, currently not more than about £64,000 per year for a maximum of three years and rarely less than £5,600. If a consortium is formed with a non-governmental organisation from a different member state, the grant may be doubled to a maximum of £128,000 (though in practice consortium projects involving fewer than three member states are virtually excluded). Its contribution may cover, for example, the purchase of equipment, salaries and allowances, materials production costs, etc. As for projects in developing countries, the other half has to be provided by your organisation and/or other donors and can include a proportion of salaries, including the value of voluntary labour used in the project. At least 15 per cent should come from the organisation's own funds or from other non-governmental sources within the EC. A small percentage (6 per cent maximum) may cover administrative costs.

In 1988 a type of block grant (known as a 'multi-projects programme') was introduced for organisations with a track record of development education co-financing, to finance small projects carried out mainly by other small NGOs or grass-roots groups.

How to apply

The details of making an application, as well as the official conditions for co-financing, are contained in *General Conditions for the Co-financing of Projects to Raise Public Awareness of Development Issues*. The same general advice applies as for co-financing projects in developing countries (see ss 10.6.1).

10.6.3 EDF micro-projects

NGOs may also receive funding for micro-projects in ACP countries under the European Development Fund (EDF). The aims are similar to those of 'co-financed' projects, but projects must be based on an initiative from the local community which is to receive the aid and approved by the national government.

The EDF can fund up to three-quarters of the cost of each project, which may not exceed a total cost of £240,000 at present, and provides technical assistance. Apply to Mr Houdart on 010 32 2 299 2802.

10.6.4 Food Aid

The role of voluntary organisations in dispensing Community food aid or goods paid for from the EC disaster fund is becoming more clearly defined. The Food Aid Division operates a special annual programme for NGOs, through an NGO liaison officer, and applications should be made by 30 September, 15 January or 30 June for allocation three months later and mobilisation and delivery after that (up to 4–5 months). There are possibilities for local and regional purchase, which cuts the time delays. Emergency food aid applications are processed more speedily.

The budgets for food aid have now been split into emergency food aid and ongoing food aid. (For details about the former see ss 10.6.5.) The ongoing food aid fund is available to look after needs which are both foreseeable and can be programmed. An increased emphasis is to be placed on rehabilitation and 'self help'. The aid is fully funded by the EC. NGOs can obtain application forms from EURONAID, PO Box 12, NL-250L, The Hague, Netherlands, Tel: 010 31 70 330 5757; Fax: 010 31 70 364 1701. Brussels contact is Mr A Reithinger, Tel: 010 32 2 299 9857. Applications must be received before 31 October if they are to be considered for the following year.

Storage and early warning programme

Funds are available for storage or early warning programmes implemented by NGOs which are better able to assess the food situation and therefore more effectively target aid. Aid can also be granted for storage programmes, which can finance activities such as the building or renovation of warehouses or food preservation costs. The cost of projects should be between 50,000 and 400,000 ecu. The total funding for 1993 is 6.3 million ecu. Contact A Reithinger, Tel: 010 32 2 299 9860.

Purchase and transport of food products

In 1993 5 million ecu is available for purchasing and transporting food products and seeds to developing countries. NGO projects must be co-funded with a minimum NGO contribution of 20,000 ecu. The costs of distribution in the field are not covered. Contact A. Reithinger, tel: 010 32 2 299 9860.

10.6.5 Emergency aid

Large sums are available through ECHO, the Commission's humanitarian aid office, to help people in developing countries facing emergencies. An increasing proportion of this is being channelled through NGOs; this proportion reached 42 per cent in 1991 compared with one-third in 1982 and only a quarter in 1981 although realistically over three-quarters of this aid is through French, Dutch and Belgian – rather than UK – NGOs. It is important to apply quickly since the Commission usually takes its decisions within three days of a disaster's occurrence. To be eligible, NGOs must prove they have the experience and resources required and already operate in the area where the emergency has occurred. NGOs normally use the funding for medicines, food, clothes and shelter. ECHO's procedures now seem to be evolving towards contracting out work to 'partner' NGOs.

While they will now under some circumstances advance some funds, they will not cover administrative costs. Much emphasis is placed on visibility of the aid and publicity. The application should explain the type of disaster and give a preliminary estimate of the number of people needing help, details of the operations the NGO proposes to carry out and, where appropriate, details of the local partner.

As a consequence of the pressure of the famine in Africa in the mid 1980s, the application process was decentralised to the delegates in a number of the worst affected countries but the decision making process is now very clearly in Brussels. European NGOs should send their application to the local Commission delegation as well as to DG VIII. For non-food emergency aid (including food aid) to ACP countries, eastern Europe, Indonesia, Philippines and Thailand, contact Mr G Molinier, Tel: 010 32 2 299 3246, and for emergency aid to other countries (including emergency food aid) contact Mr Chiarini, Tel: 010 32 2 295 4379.

It is useful to make prior contact in the case of emergency aid with VOICE (Voluntary Organisations in Co-operation in Emergencies), an NGO body within the Liaison Committee structure, which assists and co-ordinates NGO applications (10 Square Ambiorix, 1040 Brussels, Tel: 010 32 2 732 7137; Fax: 010 32 2 732 1934).

10.6.6 Refugees, returnees and displaced persons

In Asia and Latin America

Since 1984 aid has been granted to enable refugees in Asia and Latin America to become integrated and self-sufficient in the host country or to return, voluntarily, and resettle in their country of origin. The intention is to help refugees after the emergency relief stage but before long-term integration and to help with their long-term development needs. Eligible measures include providing the means of production for crop farming, livestock farming, or fisheries and crafts as well as basic infrastructure and training to meet immediate but also long-term needs. Local human and material resources should be used wherever possible. NGOs do not usually receive full funding and generally overheads cannot be covered. Requests for funding should be drawn up in line with the *General Conditions for Co-financing of Projects Undertaken in Developing Countries by Non-governmental Organisations*. The department responsible for refugees is DG I, the Commission, rue de la Loi 200, 1049 Brussels and the contacts are Mr Scanno for Central America, Tel: 010 32 2 299 2632, and Mr Mac Crea for Asia, Tel: 010 32 2 299 0810.

In the ACP countries

The purpose of this aid is the same except that the refugees must have crossed an international border. Operations to meet acute needs not covered by emergency aid can be funded in the short term but must be replaced as soon as possible by long-term operations. Wherever possible, both refugees and the local community should be directly involved.

Proposals must be endorsed by the National Authorising Officer of the ACP state concerned. Full funding, with the exception, normally, of administrative expenditure, is available to NGOs. The funding comes under the Lomé Convention so application forms are dealt with by the local Commission delegation and by DG VIII, Unit 4, at the Commission, rue de la Loi 200, 1049, Brussels. The contact is Mr Houdart, Tel: 010 32 2 299 2802.

Kurdish refugees

This fund has been recently created specifically for NGOs. It has not yet been allocated any money, but this will take place 'as soon as specific needs have been determined in the field'. This could happen during 1993. Interested NGOs can send a short letter to Mr B Ryelandt, DG VIII, Building Astrid, Brussels.

10.6.7 South Africa

Under the EC's special programme, £72 million (90 million ecu) is available for 1993 to help the victims of apartheid, to promote training, education, social assistance and humanitarian and legal aid activities in South Africa. The aid is channelled through the South African Council of Churches, the Southern African Catholic Bishops Conference, the Kagiso Trust and the trade unions. They identify the projects and present them to the Commission through a partner European NGO which has experience in South Africa. Full funding as well as co-funding can be provided. In the case of the Kagiso Trust, projects are passed through the NGO standing committee. Further information is available from Mr Hougmann, DG VIII, Tel: 010 32 2 299 3267.

10.6.8 Southern Africa

In 1993, around £12 million (15 million ecu) has been allocated to a fund created to aid victims of South Africa's destabilisation policies in the Front Line states and the Southern African Development Co-ordination Conference (SADCC). Projects can be identified by European NGOs and may be fully funded. They may, for example, assist displaced persons and orphans after conflict, provide education and training for South African refugees or support trade union training projects. Apply to Mr Houtmann, DG VIII, the Commission, rue de la Loi 200, 1049 Brussels, Tel: 010 32 2 299 3267.

10.6.9 West Bank and Gaza

The sum of £12 million (15 million ecu) has been allocated for 1993 to assist Palestinians in parts of the occupied territories not covered by any co-operation agreement between the EC and neighbouring states. Full funding as well as co-funding is available. Projects will receive priority if they increase local production capacity, create jobs and strengthen local Palestinian institutions. the EC finalises the list of projects to be financed by this fund in March. In order to be included applications must be received before the previous December. European or Palestinian NGOs may apply to Mr Jesse, 03/48, DG I at the Commission, rue de la Loi 200, 1049 Brussels, Tel: 010 32 2 299 2313.

10.6.10 Chile

There is also aid specifically available for European or Chilean NGOs working with the needy in Chile, 4.8 million ecu (£3.8 million) in 1993. Full funding is available, but co-financing is preferable. The length of the proposed action cannot exceed one year. Contact Mr Ryelandt on 010 32 2 299 9861.

10.6.11 Vietnam

To finance NGO activities in Vietnam in areas such as health education, resettlement or training 2 million ecu (£1.6 million) are available. Preference is given to financing activities in the inland provinces. Applications should be sent to Mr B Ryelandt, NGO Unit, DG VIII, rue de la Loi 200, 1049 Brussels, Tel: 010 32 2 299 9861 with a copy to Mr E Wilkinson, South East Asia Unit, DG VIII, rue de la Loi 200, 1049 Brussels, Tel: 010 32 2 299 2332. There is no special form.

10.6.12 Cambodia

In 1993 1 million ecu (£800,000) is available for projects in areas such as agriculture, rural development, education and health, compared with only 0.5 million ecu in 1992. Contact Mr B Ryelandt, Tel: 010 32 2 299 9861.

10.6.13 Migration in the Mediterranean countries

This fund was originally intended for the creation of an observatory of migratory movements. Now, it is available for projects that give a clearer picture of, and reduce, the pressures leading to migration: training activities, employment creation, integration of young people and so on. Finance is mainly for measures in the Mediterranean Countries but projects can be linked with an action in Europe generally. Apply to Mr J P Jesse, DG I, Tel: 010 32 2 299 2313. There is no special form.

10.6.14 Population policies in developing countries

In 1993 4 million ecu (£3.2 million) is available to aid the implementation and evaluation of population programmes in developing countries. Since 1990, the fund has been used to finance activities in Mediterranean countries. The funds are open to NGOs, both local and European, and cover information and awareness-raising in the field of birth control, the improvement of health services for mothers and children, training and education of women, raising awareness of the role of women and research. Special attention is given to small, innovative projects. More details about eligibility and financing can be obtained from Mr J P Jesse, DG I, Tel: 010 32 2 299 2313.

10.6.15 AIDS control in developing countries

In 1993 £8 million has been allocated to projects aimed at preventing the spread of AIDS in non-ACP developing countries as well as to awareness and information campaigns. An additional budget line has recently been set up which enables significantly more aid to be provided for programmes in ACP countries; £40 million has been allocated for a five-year period. Further information is available from Mr Kratz, DG VIII, the Commission, rue de la Loi 200, 1049 Brussels, Tel: 010 32 2 299 3098 or the Aids Task Force, 67a rue Joseph II, 1040, Brussels, Tel: 010 32 2 231 1495.

10.6.16 Campaign against drug abuse

The Community has a programme of North-South co-operation against drug abuse including a contribution to the United Nations Fund for Drug Abuse Control's crop substitution programmes. Also funded are seminars, experts' studies and research and the initiation of information, awareness-raising, education, treatment and rehabilitation schemes in the context of the campaign against drug abuse. The EC may co-finance up to 85 per cent of the cost of Community NGO projects carried out jointly with local partners.

More information is available from Mr C Van der Vaeren, Tel: 010 32 2 295 1392 or Mr P Jacobs, Tel: 010 32 2 295 8923, DG I, the Commission, rue de la Loi 200, 1049 Brussels.

10.6.17 Ecology

NGO projects to manage and protect the environment and natural resources in all developing countries are eligible for full or co-funding. The 1993 budget is £20 million. Decisions are taken in February, so applications should be in by December/January. Further information is available from Mr Guerrato, DG VIII, the Commission, rue de la Loi 200, 1049 Brussels, Tel: 010 32 2 299 3205.

10.6.18 Tropical rainforests

These funds of £40 million (50 million ecu) in 1993 cover projects which promote the protection and sustainable management of tropical rainforests, especially where these have a vital global importance (such as in climate change). Importance is given to encouraging the involvement of indigenous populations in environment policy and setting up research and training resources to bolster local institutions. Contact Mr Pironio, Tel: 010 32 2 299 2576, for projects in Africa, and Mr Jacques, Tel: 010 32 2 299 1096, for Asia and Latin America.

10.6.19 Training schemes for nationals of developing countries

NGOs can apply for aid for the creation, adaptation or improvement of training courses provided by European organisations for managers in developing countries; £1.6 million was set aside for 1992. Further information is available from Mr Amat Armengol (Tel: 010 32 2 299 3212) or Ms Neves (Tel: 010 32 2 299 2538) at DG I, the Commission, rue de la Loi 200, 1049 Brussels.

10.6.20 Women in development

Funds are available to help ensure that gender issues are more adequately addressed in development co-operation. The funds (1.5 million ecu for 1993) are used to make project officers and others involved in development co-operation more aware of issues concerning women in development, to help less developed countries analyse their policies and practices in this field, and to help set up Women in Development units in ministries in developing countries. NGOs can apply for funding only for awareness raising activities such as research, publications and seminars. The fund does not finance projects in the field. For developing countries in Asia, Latin America and the Mediterranean contact Ms E Hernandez, DG I, Tel: 010 32 2 299 0739 and for Africa, the Caribbean and the Pacific contact Ms Chapman, DG I, Tel: 010 32 2 295 0030.

10.6.21 Aid to European institutes training scientific and technical managers from developing countries

See under 9.4.2.

10.6.22 Prize for work on development

The King Baudouin Foundation, based in Brussels, awards an International Development Prize to people or organisations who make a contribution towards third world development. Its current workload includes agriculture in Africa. The Foundation's address is 21 Brederodestraat, 1000 Brussels, Tel: 010 32 2 511 1840.

10.6.23 Scientific research and co-operation

The EC funds research and development designed to benefit the developing countries, concentrating particularly on food and health; for example, improvements in agricultural production of all kinds, water resources and use, soil protection and management, rural engineering, mechanisation, product conservation, processing of products, growing and production systems, tropical diseases, appropriate health care systems and nutrition. See the Commission handbook, *EC Research Funding*. Projects are carried out through shared-cost contracts bringing together scientists from the EC and from developing countries. Further information is available from DG XII, Science, Research and Development at the Commission, rue de la Loi 200, 1049 Brussels.

10.6.24 Loans from the European Investment Bank

Information about loans for work in developing countries is available from the European Investment Bank, 100 Boulevard Konrad Adenauer 2950, Luxembourg, Tel: 010 352 43791.

10.6.25 Scholarships for overseas students

See ss 9.4.2, 'Students from the African, Caribbean and Pacific countries'.

10.6.26 Aid to humanitarian organisations

See s 8.4.

10.7 Central and eastern Europe

10.7.1 The PHARE programme

With 1,040 million ecu (£830 million) in 1993, the PHARE programme finances EC assistance for the restructuring of the economies of Albania, Baltic countries, ex-Yugoslavia, Romania, Bulgaria, Czech Republic, Slovakia, Hungary, Poland.

Many UK NGOs also obtain funding from the related British-funded Charities Know-how fund, which has awarded 300 grants so far totalling just under £1 million. Further information from Ian Bell or Clare Walters, Tel: 071 831 7798.

Within the PHARE programme some resources (15 per cent in 1992) are earmarked for humanitarian aid. This category includes both emergency aid and longer term humanitarian aid. There are also funds for strengthening civil society in central Europe.

Humanitarian aid

Emergency humanitarian aid is managed by ECHO (see 10.6.5). Longer-term humanitarian aid is managed within the PHARE programme. Humanitarian aid programmes are currently being financed in Romania, Bulgaria and Albania. Some of these programmes are intended specifically for NGOs (for example, support to NGO projects in Albania); in other cases (for example, support for child protection policy in Romania) there are more medium-term macroeconomic programmes where NGOs can become involved, but under much more rigid conditions.

NGO operations in Albania

A special fund of 2 million ecu (£1.6 million) finances NGO activities to aid the disadvantaged in Albania. This fund is to support short-term projects to cover immediate needs. Projects can range between 75,000 and 200,000 ecu. Funding is by co-financing (see 10.6.1). The fund is managed by the UNDP in Tirana on behalf of the EC Commission. Funding applications must therefore be sent to the UNDP delegate in Tirana, with a copy to Ms M Houben, DGI/E/5, the Commission, rue de la Loi 200, 1049 Brussels, Tel: 010 32 2 299 1931.

UNDP: Mr J N Marchal, Resident Representative, Tirana, Albania, Tel: 010 355 42 331 22; Fax: 010 355 42 344 48.

The former Yugoslavia

Since the beginning of the conflict in 1991, the Community has contributed 290 million ecu (£232 million) in humanitarian aid for war victims in former

Yugoslavia, to cope with food and support facilities for some three million refugees. The Community provided a further 162.5 million ecus for the first six months of 1992. The UN and non-governmental agencies act as distributors. Further information from the European Communities' Humanitarian Office (ECHO): contact Mr Chiarini, Tel: 010 32 2 295 4379.

10.8 Key publications

ACP.EEC joint assembly, shared democracy, European Parliament, available free from its London office, 2 Queen Anne's Gate, London SW1H 9AA, Tel: 071-222 0411; Fax: 071-222 2713

Aid from the European Community, Trade and the European Community, Food and the European Community, series of leaflets outlining effects of EC policy on the third world, 1990, 4pp, from World Development Movement, 25 Beehive Place, London SW9 7QR, Tel: 071-737 6215

Antenna, published bi-monthly by the European Ecumenical Organisation for Development, 1040 Brussels, Tel: 010 32 2 230 6105

The Community and its Eastern Neighbours, Europe on the Move series, available from the Commission, 8 Storey's Gate, London SW1P 3AT, Tel: 071-973 1992; Fax: 071-973 1900

The Courier: Africa, Caribbean, Pacific-European Community, published every two months by the Commission and available from DG VIII, the Commission, rue de la Loi 200, 1049 Brussels

EC Research Funding – a guide for applicants, available from the London office of the European Commission, 8 Storey's Gate, London SW1P 3AT, Tel: 071-973 1992; Fax: 071-973 1900

Europa, bi-monthly, European Commission, available from the Commission, 8 Storey's Gate, London SW1P 3AT, Tel: 071-973 1992; Fax: 071-973 1900

Europe – South Dialogue, European Commission, available from the London office of the Commission, 8 Storey's Gate, London SW1P 3AT, Tel: 071-973 1992; Fax: 071-973 1900

General Conditions for Co-financing of Projects to Raise Public Awareness of Development Issues carried out by Non-governmental organisations in the European Community, European Commission, available from DG VIII, the Commission, rue de la Loi 200, 1049 Brussels

General Conditions for the Co-financing of Projects Undertaken in Developing Countries by Non-governmental Organisations, European Commission, available from DG VIII, the Commission, rue de la Loi 200, 1049 Brussels

A Guide to Successful Lobbying of the EC, by Ed Mayo, 1992, 32pp, from World Development Movement, 25 Beehive Place, London SW9 7QR, Tel: 071-737 6215

Humanitarian Aid from the European Community, Europe on the Move series, available free from the Commission, 8 Storey's Gate, London SW1P 3AT, Tel: 071-973 1992, Fax: 071-973 1900

NGDO-EC News, (see especially the spring issue, *Digest of Community Resources available for Financing and Development Activities*), a bulletin published after each meeting of the Liaison Committee of Development NGOs, Square Ambiorix 10, 1040 Brussels, Tel: 010 32 2 736 4087; Fax: 010 32 2 732 1934

Second World, Third World: How Changes in Eastern Europe are affecting the world's poor, by Ed Mayo, 1990, 30pp, from World Development Movement, 25 Beehive Place, London SW9 7QR, Tel: 071-737 6215

Towards a New World Partnership, European Parliament, available free from London office, 2 Queen Anne's Gate, London SW1H 9AA, tel: 071-222 0411; Fax: 071-222 2713

11 Environment

This chapter will be of interest to environmental pressure and action groups, those involved in the nuclear debate, the consumer lobby, industry, the trade unions and local authorities.

11.1 Key Commission departments

Environment, civil protection and nuclear safety: Directorate-General XI

Commissioner: Ioannis Paloekrassas (Greek)

Key officials: Laurens Jan Brinkhorst (Dutch), director-general responsible for protection and improvement of the environment, Tel: 010 32 2 299 2254; Claus Stuffmann (German, speaks English), deals with natural resources, economic aspects, action relating to the environment, public awareness, Tel: 010 32 2 296 9506.

Energy: Directorate-General XVII

Commissioner: Abel Matutes (Spanish)

Director-General: Mr C. Maniatopoulous (Greek, speaks some English)

Key officials: Jean-Claude Guibal, energy policy, Tel: 010 32 2 295 9445; Mr De Bauw (Belgian), strategy, dissemination and evaluation, Tel: 010 32 2 295 4122; Fabrizio Caccia Dominioni (Italian, speaks English), director, nuclear energy, rational use of energy, Tel: 010 32 2 295 2410.

11.2 Extent of EC involvement

While protection of the environment is not mentioned in the original Treaty of Rome, the Single European Act amending the European treaties devotes a whole chapter to environmental policy. A key article says that environmental criteria should be integrated with all policies. The Maastricht Treaty expands these commitments to include town and country planning, land use, water and energy supplies.

The EC already has extensive environmental legislation ranging from drinking and bathing water quality, to protection of wild birds, limits on car and aircraft noise levels, the fitting of catalytic converters to all new cars and stabilisation of carbon dioxide emissions at 1990 levels by the year 2000 (although there are serious doubts over the likelihood of even this limited target being achieved). There is also a proposal for an EC energy tax on carbon fuels. A voluntary environment-friendly labelling system has been established, as has a voluntary eco-audit scheme for the business community, and the Corine programme is improving the comparability of EC environmental statistics and data. The introduction of majority voting on more issues as well as heightened public awareness of environmental problems is likely to force the UK to upgrade its environmental protection.

11.2.1 The Blue Flag Scheme

The Blue Flag Scheme run by the Foundation for Environmental Education in Europe (FEEE) was started in 1987, the European Year of the Environment. Blue flags are awarded in three categories: ports, pleasure-boats and, the most important category, beaches. The award for beaches includes the quality of the water and the coastline, the management and safety of the bathing areas and public education and information. They must obviously comply with EC legislation on the quality of bathing water.

11.3 Key people

11.3.1 In Britain

Richard Longman, Environmental Protection, Central Division, Room A132, Department of the Environment, Romney House, 43 Marsham Street SW1P 3PY, Tel: 071-276 8146

Robert Elphick, London office of the Commission, 8 Storey's Gate, London SW1P 3AT, Tel: 071-973 1992; Fax: 071-973 1900

Nigel Haigh, Institute for European Environmental Policy, 158 Buckingham Palace Road, London SW1W 9TR, Tel: 071-388 2117. The Institute is based in Bonn, Paris, Brussels, Arnhem and London. It studies environmental policy making in Europe.

For an up-to-date list of members of the Environment, Public Health and Consumer Affairs Committee, contact the London office of the European Parliament. The chairman is Kenneth Collins (Labour), 11 Stuarton Park, East Kilbride G74 4LA, Tel: 03552-37282.

11.3.2 At EC level

Raymond van Ermen, Secretary General, European Environmental Bureau (EEB), rue de la Victoire, 1060 Brussels, Tel: 010 32 2 539 0037

UK contact: Julie Hill, Green Alliance, 49 Wellington Street, London WC2E 7BN, Tel: 071-836 0341. Alternatively contact: Fiona Reynolds, Council for the Protection of Rural England, Warwick House, 25 Buckingham Palace Road, London SW1W 0PP, Tel: 071-976 6433; Fax: 071-976 6373.

The EEB is a coalition of about 150 NGOs concerned about the environment in the European Community. It provides its members with information and represents them on EC issues. It has a small office in Brussels.

European Environment Agency

This agency, which was created at the end of 1989, collects environmental data and statistics on air, water, soil, natural resources, waste management, noise, dangerous substances and protection of the coastline so that real cross-Europe comparisons can be made.

11.4 Current EC issues

The fifth environmental action programme was published in April 1992, and shows a shift in strategy from corrective action to preventive measures. It emphasises the need for the rational use of resources, involving a decrease in production, a more efficient use of products followed by their re-use or recycling where possible. Energy efficiency and waste management are given particular importance.

11.5 Funding

The EC is paying increasing attention to environmental needs, but the amount of money available for projects is not large. The European Social Fund (see ss 3.4.1) has been used to train workers in building conservation and to employ people to clear derelict land. Support for agriculture includes aids to improve farm efficiency, help to farmers, compensatory allowances payable in mountain and less-favourable agricultural areas and aids to agricultural marketing and processing. Environmental, afforestation and early retirement measures were introduced in the 1992 CAP reform. The Regional Development Fund (see ss 3.4.6) has been used to restore historic buildings for tourism, to create pedestrian areas and to improve industrial dereliction.

It could in theory also be used for parks, nature reserves and railway preservation. Sewage works, which reduce water pollution, schemes to recycle or incinerate waste, and energy-saving projects have also received aid under the Regional Development Fund. For example, the National Trust was awarded £40,200 for the purchase and installation of a windmatic electricity generator on Lundy Island.

11.5.1 EC Financial instrument for the environment (LIFE)

The LIFE programme replaces ACNAT, MEDSPA and NORSPA, and ties in with the EC Fifth Action Programme relating to the environment, 'Towards Sustainability'. There are five categories under which funding is available (on a competitive basis) towards 'priority environmental actions':

(i) promotion of sustainable development and the quality of the environment (eg innovatory demonstration technologies in target industrial sectors, recycling, rehabilitation of contaminated land, models for integrating environmental concerns into land use planning and management and socio-economic sectors);

(ii) protection of habitats and nature (eg contributing to the implementation of the Birds Directive and Habitats Directive);

(iii) administrative structures and environment services (eg environmental monitoring networks);

(iv) education, training and information; and

(v) action outside community territory (ie in the Mediterranean or Baltic regions).

Demonstration projects, awareness campaigns and actions providing incentives and technical assistance are the types of projects eligible for funding. Schemes should be of Community interest, contributing to the execution of its environmental policy, respect the 'polluter pays' principle and foresee a dissemination of their results. Research is not eligible for funding, and neither are feasibility studies, conferences or seminars unless they form an integral part of the proposed project. The Community will fund up to 30 per cent of costs for schemes involving income generation, 100 per cent of costs for actions assisting Commission initiatives and 50 per cent for all other projects. In exceptional cases 75 per cent may be given to actions relating to the protection of species, habitats or biotopes. The budget allocated to the end of 1995 is 400 million ecu (£320 million).

For further information contact Richard Longman, Room A132, Department of the Environment, Romney House, 43 Marsham Street, London SW1P 3PY, Tel: 071-276 8146.

11.5.2 Common Agricultural Policy

The Common Agricultural Policy (CAP) is a key influence on land-use management, and hence on nature conservation in the EC. The high level of agricultural support under the CAP has led to intensification and specialisation within agriculture and consequently to the loss of wildlife habitats and pollution. Some agricultural schemes have been introduced which are beneficial to the environment, such as the Environmentally Sensitive Areas (ESAs), and the agri-environment action plan.

Agri-environment schemes

As part of the 1992 CAP reform settlement, a new agri-environment regulation was agreed. This means that, for the first time, all member states of the Community are required to draw up programmes offering incentives to farmers to manage their land in an environmentally beneficial way. At the time of going to press, MAFF (the Ministry of Agriculture, Fisheries and Food) is conducting public consultation on its proposals for new environmental incentive schemes in England. These proposals will develop and extend the existing range of environmental incentives available to farmers. They are expected to be open for application, in most cases, during 1993/4. The schemes should encourage organic farming, extensification, environmentally beneficial management of farmland and upkeep of abandoned land, setting aside farmland for at least 20 years for environmental purposes so creating or improving wildlife habitats, improving semi-natural moorland vegetation and creating access on Environmentally Sensitive Areas and set-aside land.

Environmentalists have pointed out that environmental spending on agriculture would still amount only to 2.5 per cent of the total outlay. The need remains, therefore, for more fundamental reform of the CAP, shifting resources from price support to environmental management.

Agricultural Guidance Fund

A small proportion of CAP funds is allocated to direct aid to agriculture such as schemes for infrastructure and agricultural development in 'less-favoured areas' to prevent rural de-population. Environmental groups believe that these schemes sometimes can do more harm than good to the environment by encouraging overuse of land and the destruction of natural areas by, for example, draining of wetlands, but you may just be able to launch a scheme which benefits both the environment and local farmers.

Subsidies may also help with special training or the creation of pilot projects which could, for example, promote the marketing of biologically grown food. Applications should be sent to the local office of the Ministry of Agriculture, Fisheries and Food (MAFF).

Environmentally Sensitive Areas

The British scheme, co-financed by the EC under the Structural Fund, compensates for loss of income by farmers who preserve the environment in Environmentally Sensitive Areas. This has been extended to cover tourism and diversification in a total of seven counties of Eastern England. MAFF have proposed to set up six new ESAs, which would bring the total to 22 in England. Funding for the scheme will be increased by £12 million over three years. Instead of paying compensation for loss of income, there have been suggestions to pay for positive measures such as planting hedgerows. MAFF proposes to open suitable ESA farmland for new public access.

Set-aside

Following agreement on the reform of the Common Agricultural Policy (CAP) in 1992, the old five-year set-aside scheme and the associated Countryside Premium Scheme are now closed to new applicants, although existing participants in these schemes continue to manage their land according to the scheme rules until their agreements come to an end.

As a result of the reform of the CAP, most arable farmers are now required to set-aside 15 per cent of their arable area if they wish to receive EC support payments on their arable crops. Set-aside is intended to help reduce over-production of arable crops and bring down the costs of the CAP. The result can be more intensive use of the remaining land. However, set-aside can also provide opportunities for farmers to manage their set-aside land in environmentally beneficial ways, for example by creating a habitat attractive to wildlife, or by encouraging rare arable flora. From 1993 these opportunities will be increased with the introduction of arrangements under which farmers will be able to keep the same land in set-aside for longer periods. Farmers are also entitled to grow crops for non-food use, such as biomass on their set-aside land. MAFF provides advice to farmers on environmentally positive ways of managing their set-aside land. Further information from Cereals and Set-aside Division, MAFF, Whitehall Place, London SW1, Tel: 071-270 3000.

Habitat improvement scheme

MAFF proposes to encourage the creation or improvement of a range of wildlife habitats such as coastal saltmarsh and water fringes along vulnerable watercourses, through the withdrawal of selected areas of land from agricultural production for 20 years.

Farm woodlands

Under the forestry regulation (2080/92) agreed as one of the CAP reform-accompanying measures, an EC contribution is made towards aid schemes to encourage afforestation of agricultural land which must be drawn up by member states. The Forestry Commission's Woodland Grant Scheme (WGS) and MAFF's Farm Woodland Premium Scheme (FWPS) will form the basis of the UK's national programme. The WGS offers grants towards the costs of establishing woodland while the FWPS makes available annual payments up to £250/hectare for 10–15 years to farmers establishing woodland on agricultural land under the WGS to help abate the agricultural income foregone. Further information on the WGS is available from local Forestry Conservancy Offices and the FWPS from MAFF Regional Services Centres.

Extensification

Grants are available to farmers to farm less intensively, specifying that production must not increase. Appropriate waste management and the creation and maintenance of traditional features such as hedgerows, rows of trees, dry stone walls and water courses are encouraged. Hitherto unimproved grasslands and other habitats must not be disturbed. Under MAFF's agri-environment package, a new moorland scheme would be established to encourage a reduction in the number of livestock grazing moorland outside the ESAs where this can result in improvement in heather, other semi-natural vegetation and associated wildlife habitats. Further information is available from MAFF.

Organic farming

MAFF is proposing to introduce aids for farmers who undertake to introduce or continue with organic farming methods. During the early phase of conversion a higher rate of aid would be paid for two years on each parcel of land put into conversion; thereafter a lower rate would be payable for three years. Rates would be lower in the less-favoured areas because of their more extensive production methods.

Countryside stewardship

The Countryside Commission, funded by the DOE, is piloting the countryside stewardship scheme to protect and enhance valued English landscapes and habitats and to improve the opportunities for the public enjoyment of the countryside. This scheme, which now covers over 30,000 hectares (over 115 square miles) targets chalk and limestone grassland, lowland heath, waterside landscapes, coastal land and uplands. In 1992 it was also extended to historic landscapes and old meadows and pasture. It is not limited to farmers, is testing a number of new approaches and is complementary to the ESAs.

Sites of Specific Scientific Interest

On designated Sites of Special Scientific Interest (SSSIs), the Government's nature conservation agency, English Nature, may provide payment for adopting particular management practices to protect a habitat or species. Such agreements currently cover approximately 45,000 hectares (175 square miles). In some SSSIs a wildlife enhancement scheme has been introduced to achieve further benefits for wildlife.

Farm and conservation grant scheme

This scheme, which is run by MAFF, provides grants for pollution control equipment and for environmental improvements such as hedge planting. Expenditure is forecast at £35 million in 1995-6. Grants are available to help farmers meet the cost of fencing off woods to protect them from stock, to provide, improve or replace traditional walls and banks and to repair or reinstate farm buildings using traditional materials.

11.5.3 Transport

The EC's fifth Environmental Action Programme (which covers the period 1993-2000) and its Green Paper on the impact of transport on the environment have both emphasised the importance of integrating environmental concerns into areas of policy and planning, with the maximum involvement of all the interested parties. The Community is responsible for individual legislative measures dealing with exhaust emissions and noise pollution because of the need to prevent distortions within the single market caused by differences in environmental controls on businesses.

There is an action programme proposed for 1993-4 to achieve more competitive, efficient and environmentally friendly transport services. A White Paper on the Community's policy has also been drawn up. The Maastricht Treaty includes a proposal for trans-European networks, covering telecommunications as well as road and rail routes, with the aim of improving important cross-European links.

The Common Transport Policy aims to go beyond measures to reduce pollution such as energy efficiency, tighter emission standards, tougher inspection and maintenance requirements, reducing congestion, noise monitoring and increasing safety standards for the transport of dangerous goods. It aims also to assess the pattern of demand for transport, to increase the efficiency of existing transport networks and to make use of collective and environmentally friendlier transport. It wants local schemes which encourage walking or the use of bicycles to be developed, especially in urban areas.

11.5.4 Protection of the architectural heritage

See ss 9.5.2.

11.5.5 Projects involving co-operation with other member states

Environmental activities of a 'multinational character and European inspiration' are eligible for funding by the European Cultural Foundation. You must work with organisations or individuals in at least two other European countries. See ss 9.4.1, 'Activities relevant to the EC' for more information.

11.5.6 European Foundation for the Improvement of Living and Working Conditions

This foundation, based in Dublin, has a small budget for research, seminars, working groups, courses, conferences and pilot studies aimed at improving living and working conditions. It has tended to concentrate on working conditions but there is movement now towards looking at the wider environment. Administered by a board of government, trade union and employer representatives, its activities tend to be aimed at industry and the unions rather than voluntary organisations. Its current workload covers industrial relations and participation, restructuring working life, promoting health and safety, protecting the environment, the worker and the public, raising the standard and quality of life for all, and new technologies. All studies are commissioned, usually from academic institutions. However, if you suggest a project that comes within its current interests, you may be lucky and receive help. Its work programme has included themes such as the urban environment, including living conditions of the long-term un-employed and initiatives linked to voluntary work concerning the environment, and the effects of biotechnology on the environment and non-nuclear wastes. Write for a free annual report and information dossier to see whether any of its future projects are appropriate for you: European Foundation for the Improvement of Living and Working Conditions, Loughlinstown House, Shankhill, Co Dublin, Ireland, Tel: 010 353 1 282 6888; Fax: 010 353 1 282 6456.

11.5.7 King Baudouin Foundation

Another long shot for funding is the Brussels-based King Baudouin Foundation. Although its aims are primarily related to Belgium, it has sponsored seminars and research projects by the European Environmental Bureau on the relationship between agricultural and environmental objectives. Its current interests are social issues, the environment and land-use planning. The King Baudouin Foundation is at 21 Brederodestraat, 1000 Brussels, Tel: 010 32 2 511 1840.

11.5.8 Scientific research into the environment

The current EC research and development programme (1990-4) has been allocated 5.7 billion ecu (£4.5 billion) of which 9 per cent is for research into the environment. This includes monitoring the effects of pollution, chemicals, effects of human activities on the environment, environmental processes and ecosystems, waste management, technologies to reduce and prevent pollution and restoration of damaged environments. Anyone can participate in the programme (universities, industrial companies, private and public research institutes), but at least one other partner from another member state is usually a prerequisite. The work must not be geared, directly or indirectly, to the creation of new products or processes for the marketplace. Other necessary criteria include scientific and technical originality, technical competence and a sound financial plan (about 50 per cent of the project should be self-financing).

Tenders for projects appear in the *Official Journal of the European Communities*. This can be obtained from the Office for Official Publications of the EC, 2 Rue Mercier, L-2985, Luxembourg, Tel: 010 352 49 9281. The time available for the submitting of a proposal is usually about three months, but can be as short as six weeks. The Commission cannot give longer deadlines as the number of applications is very high, so ensure that the proposal is sent before the deadline. If this is not possible, it is better to wait for the next call.

For more information contact Heinrich Ott, Research and Development Directorate-General XII at the Commission's Brussels office, Tel: 010 32 2 295 1182; Fax: 010 32 2 296 3024, or consult the Commission's handbook *EC Research Funding*.

11.5.9 Projects to increase awareness

A small sum (4.55 million ecu) is available for positive action to educate and increase the awareness of the public about environmental problems, by means of campaigns, exhibitions, competitions, publications and training courses. Both national and regional organisations may apply. Funding averages around 150,000 ecu and generally provides between 10 and 50 per cent of the costs of the project. Priority is given to projects benefiting the Mediterranean region and central and eastern europe. Projects should generate a marked Community-wide multiplier effect, have a direct trans-frontier impact, bring about a lasting change in the behaviour of the partners involved, entail effective co-operation between the different partners, and fit in with the priorities of the EC's environment programme. Proposals should be sent to H Jankowski, Commission of the European Communities, rue de la Loi 200, 1049 Brussels.

11.5.10 Environmental education and training

About 1 million ecu (£800,000) is available for 1993 to finance projects to integrate environmental protection into education and training pro-grammes. Particular emphasis will be placed this year on all activities relating to teacher training. Proposals should be sent to H Jankowski, Commission of the European Communities, rue de la Loi 200, 1049 Brussels.

11.5.11 Coastal environment

The Commission has adopted a programme to improve the coastal environment in the least developed regions of the Community, which include Northern Ireland. Funding, set at £320 million (400 million ecu) for 1990-3, comes from the ERDF (see ss 3.4.6). The ENVIREG programme (Programme of Regional Action on the Initiative of the Commission concerning the Environment) will help finance projects such as water treatment, sewage treatment and disposal, storage and recycling of hazardous and toxic wastes, land-use planning, feasibility studies and vocational training. The Commission intends to bring forward a similar programme to deal with environmental problems along the Atlantic Ocean and the Baltic, Irish and North Seas.

11.5.12 Animal welfare

There is no longer a separate budget to support European animal protection organisations, seminars, training operations and pilot schemes. However such organisations may submit schemes under the LIFE programme (see para 11.5.1). Contact: Jaime Rubal Rodriguez DGXI, the Commission, rue de la Loi 200, 1049 Brussels, Tel: 010 32 2 299 0045.

11.5.13 Rural development

The 400 million ecu (£320 million) LEADER programme runs from 1990 to 1993 but may be continued. It stands for the liaison between actions for the development of the rural economy. The programme will support the organisation of rural development, vocational training, rural tourism, small firms, craft enterprises, local services and the exploitation and marketing of agricultural projects in Objective 1 and 5b areas (see ss 3.4.6). Support goes to local groups based on voluntary organisations, local authorities or a combination of the two. Further information from Yves Champetier, AEIDL, 260 Chaussée St Pierre, 1040 Brussels, Tel: 010 32 2 736 4960; Fax: 010 32 2 736 0434.

11.5.14 European Investment Bank

The bank provides loans on favourable terms to help finance investment projects which foster the Community's balanced development. EIB-funded projects must comply with EC directives concerning the environment, and the EIB monitors the effect of the projects to ensure that this is so. To minimise adverse environmental effects further it finds promoters of, and invites companies to tender for, the installation of systems to protect the environment. It also issues loans for projects directly aiming to protect the environment. Eligible projects include those dealing with the economic development of the less-favoured regions and urban renewal projects, improvements in transport and telecommunications, action to safeguard and improve the environment, increasing the competitiveness of industry in the Community, improving the security of energy supplies to help reach the Community's energy policy objectives, and any small or medium-sized enterprises in the industrial (including tourism), agricultural and fisheries sectors.

The New Community Instrument (NCI) also provides loans for projects involving small and medium-sized businesses, including those relating to the environment, new technologies and the rational use of energy, sometimes jointly with the EIB. The EIB's address is 100 Boulevard Konrad Adenauer, 2950 Luxembourg, Tel: 010 352 43791; or 68 Pall Mall, London SW1Y 5ES, Tel: 071-839 3351.

11.5.15 Biotechnology

Biotechnology – applying scientific and engineering principles to the processing of materials by biological agents to produce goods and services – has since long ago brought us wines and beers, breads and cheeses. Selective breeding produced the high yielding strains of rice and wheat that allowed India to become self-sufficient in grain, but brought problems such as lower resistance to some diseases and heavy dependence on fertilisers. Now genetic engineering allows the development of new properties in micro-organisms, plants and animals: a tomato that can be sold ripe but not soggy; new crops that fix nitrogen for themselves or that grow in more extreme conditions; medicines produced by organisms rather than by chemical synthesis that are compatible with the human metabolism.

The opportunities for applying the new biotechnologies to the manufacture of medical and veterinary products, to agriculture and food processing, to energy, pollution control and waste treatment are rapidly increasing. No accident has yet occurred with genetic engineering. But its history is still too short for the assessment of risk on the normal criteria of probability. Many of the most interesting techniques are very new, or still in prospect. For instance, the possible problems that could, probably very rarely, follow from the release of genetically modified organisms (GMOs) have almost no track record.

New economic problems of patenting and competition, and new ethical problems, demand public understanding, and action by the Community. The European Commission has a number of draft directives in the field of biotechnology, some of which have been adopted by the Council. One deals with safety factors and emergency procedures, another with legal protection for biotechnical inventions. There are several schemes under the EC R&D programme to promote research co-operation in biotechnology, such as BRIDGE (Biotechnical Research for Innovation, Development and Growth in Europe), which will be followed within the framework of the current R&D programme by BIOTECH, covering basic and applied biological research, and AIR (Agro-Industrial Research). Further information is available from Maurice Lex (Safety and legal aspects of biotechnical R&D, Tel: 010 32 2 296 5619). Information on biotechnical R&D related to the EC is covered in a newsletter, EBIS (European Biotechnology Information Service). Copies may be obtained free of charge from M Lex, DGXII, at the Commission's Brussels address. Information is also available from Dr I Lawrence, Laboratory of the Government Chemist, Department of Trade and Industry, Tel: 081-943 7591.

11.5.16 Commercialisation of energy saving and alternative sources of energy

The Thermie scheme is running from 1990 to 1994 to promote energy technology and provide grants for the commercialisation of innovatory projects in rational use of energy, renewable energy sources, coal and other solid fuels and hydrocarbons, and for projects that disseminate information to industry about the rational use of energy and renewable energy. Most of the funding supports projects that demonstrate new technologies with completed R&D. Grants of up to 40 per cent of project costs are available. The total budget for the programme is approximately £500 million (625 million ecu). The final call for proposals is expected in the summer of 1993, and the successor programme is already under discussion.

Further information is available from Richard Shock at Energy Technology Support Unit, Harwell Laboratory, Harwell, Oxon OX11 0RA, Tel: 0235-432621; Fax: 0235-433548. He deals with rational use of energy. Arthur Hollis at the ETSU (Tel: 0235-433561; Fax: 0235-432050) deals with renewable energy sources, Philip Sharman at the ETSU (Tel: 0235-432669; Fax: 0235-433548) deals with solid fuels, and Peter Christie at Offshore Supplies Office, Alhambra House, 45 Waterloo Street, Glasgow G2 6AT (Tel: 041-221 5760; Fax: 041-221 1718) deals with oil and gas.

11.5.17 JOULE

The Commission has funded a series of non-nuclear energy R&D programmes as part of its general research and development programme. The Joint Opportunities for Unconventional or Long-term Energy technology programme (JOULE) ran from 1989 to 1992 and was replaced by JOULE II, which will run until 1994. The latter has been allocated about £100 million to cover four sectors: (i) analysis of strategies and modelling; (ii) minimum emission power production from fossil sources; (iii) renewable energy sources and geothermal energy; and (iv) energy utilisation and conservation. Successor programmes are under discussion.

To be eligible for funding proposals have to cover pre-competitive research and to come from collaborators in at least two member states. Support is 50 per cent of eligible costs save for Higher Education Institutes where it is 100 per cent of marginal costs. For further information contact David Irving, Electricity Division, Department of Trade and Industry, 1 Palace Street, London SW1E 5HE, Tel: 071-238 3318; Fax: 071-828 7969.

11.5.18 The greenhouse effect

The Commission has accepted commitments to reinforce energy saving, improve energy efficiency, develop new energy sources and encourage the use of safe nuclear technology. It has proposed the 40 million ecu (£32 million) ALTENER programme to encourage new forms of energy and the SAVE energy conservation programme, which provides guidelines for national strategies to limit carbon dioxide emissions. An energy tax has been proposed to help achieve this goal. The ALTENER programme which would run initially for five years, from 1993 to 1997, will aid studies, support member states' initiatives, foster the creation of an information network on renewables and aid industrial action on biomass, in particular the production of biofuels. The REWARD programme covers research into the recycling of waste, including recycling technologies, and fuel and energy production from waste. For more information see *EC Research Funding*.

11.6 Key publications

Agriculture and England's environment, information on the grant schemes, from MAFF press office, Whitehall Place, London SW1A 2HH, Tel: 071-270 8973; Fax: 071-270 8443

Commission Communication on the Future Development of the Common Transport Policy, White Paper, from the European Commission, rue de la Loi 200, 1049 Brussels

EC Research Funding, EC Commission, available from its information office, 8 Storey's Gate, London SW1P 3AT, Tel: 071-973 1992; Fax: 071-973 1900

Environmental Policy in the European Community, Periodical 5/1990, EC Commission, European Documentation, obtainable from the Commission's information offices

European Community Environment Legislation, European Commission, available from DG XI, the Commission, rue de la Loi 200, 1049 Brussels

European Demonstration Projects in the Energy Field, European file series, EC Commission, available free from the Commission's information office, 8 Storey's Gate, London SW1P 3AT, Tel: 071-973 1992; Fax: 071-973 1900

The European Energy Policy, European file series, EC Commission, available free from the Commission's information office, 8 Storey's Gate, London SW1P 3AT, Tel: 071- 973 1992; Fax: 071-973 1900

European Environmental Bureau, annual reports, rue de la Victoire, 1060 Brussels, Tel: 010 32 2 539 0037

Farm and conservation grant scheme, from MAFF press office, Whitehall Place, London SW1A 2HH, Tel: 071-270 8973; Fax: 071-270 8443

Improve Your Environment Using the Financial Instruments of the European Community, European Environmental Bureau, rue de la Victoire, 1060 Brussels, Tel: 010 32 2 539 0037

Manual of Environmental Policy: The EC and Britain, by Nigel Haigh, Longman

Nature Conservation, Europe 2000, from the European Parliament, Directorate-General for Information and Public Relations, Publications and Events Division, L-2929 Luxembourg

New Vitality for the Countryside, European file series, EC Commission, available free from the Commission's information office, 8 Storey's Gate, London SW1P 3AT, Tel: 071-973 1992; Fax: 071-973 1900

Nuclear Energy in the European Community, European file series, EC Commission, available free from the Commission office, 8 Storey's gate, London SW1P 3AT, Tel: 071-973 1992; Fax: 071-973 1900

Nuclear Safety: The European Community following the Chernobyl Accident, European file series, EC Commission, available free from the Commission's office, 8 Storey's Gate, London SW1P 3AT, Tel: 071-973 1992; Fax: 071-973 1900

Pollution Knows No Frontiers, European file series, EC Commission, available free from the Commission's information office, 8 Storey's Gate, London SW1P 3AT, Tel: 071-973 1992; Fax: 071-973 1900

Protecting our Environment, European file series, EC Commission, available free from the Commission's information office, 8 Storey's Gate, London SW1P 3AT, Tel: 071-973 1992; Fax: 071-973 1900

The Public and Biotechnology, a discussion document, Eirlys Roberts, available free from the European Foundation for the Improvement of Living and Working Conditions, Loughlinstown House, Shankhill, County Dublin, Ireland (versions in English, French, Italian, Spanish and German)

Towards Sustainability, COM(92) 23 final – Volume II of 30.3.1992, available from the London Office of the Commission, 8 Storey's Gate, London SW1P 3AT, Tel: 071-973 1992; Fax: 071-973 1900

12 *Health*

This chapter is aimed at health professionals, research scientists and institutions, consumer organisations, trade unions, local authorities, social workers and voluntary organisations involved in health issues.

12.1 Key Commission departments

Medical and health research: Directorate-General XII

Public and occupational health: Directorate-General V

Commissioners: Padraig Flynn (Irish), Antonio Ruberti (Italian)

Key officials: Dr André Baert, programme manager for Biomedical and Health Research Programme (BIOMED), DG XII, EC Commission's Brussels address, Tel: 010 32 2 295 0032; Alain van Vossel, Europe against Cancer, DG V at the Commission's Brussels address, Tel: 010 32 2 296 2578; Fax: 010 32 2 296 2393; David Sweet, general information, Tel: 010 32 2 295 3909

William Hunter, head of directorate for health and safety, DG V, at the Commission, 200 rue de la Loi, 1049 Brussels, Tel: 010 32 2 296 2248.

12.2 Extent of EC involvement

From the start, a basic objective of the Community has been to achieve better living standards and better working conditions for the people of Europe. Co-operation on research and development has always been important to the EC, beginning with a 1955 scheme covering the coal and steel sectors. Further, its commitment to the free movement of workers has involved the EC in the harmonisation of health and safety standards at work. But health issues are now a greater priority for the Community, partly as a result of the Citizen's Europe initiative. The work of Directorate-General V has been expanded to include public health, AIDS toxicology, drug abuse and health problems of migrant workers. EC legislation will control the labelling, tar content and advertising of cigarettes.

The Maastricht Treaty's provision for public health gives a framework for health campaigns co-ordinated by the EC. These could include AIDS or smoking awareness campaigns, and also health research. Article 129 states: 'the Community shall contribute towards ensuring a high level of human health protection by encouraging co-operation between the member states and, if necessary, lending support to their action'. The Council has ruled out any attempts to harmonise legislation between member states in the area of health.

12.3 Key people

12.3.1 In Britain

Gillian Breen, International Section, Medical Research Council, 20 Park Crescent, London W1N 4AL

The International Affairs Officer, Coronary Prevention Group, 102 Gloucester Place, London W1H 3DA, Tel: 071-935 2889

Research Management Division, Department of Health, Alexander Fleming House, Elephant and Castle, London SE1 6BY, Tel: 071-972 4217

12.3.2 In Brussels

William Lay, Committee of Family Organisations in the European Community (COFACE), rue de Londres 17, 1050 Brussels, Tel: 010 32 2 511 4179

Xavier Schoenmaekers, International Heart Network and Andrew Hayes, European Cancer League, both at rue du Trône 98, 1040 Brussels, Tel: 010 32 2 512 9360; Fax: 010 32 2 512 6673.

12.4 Funding

12.4.1 Health and safety at work

A framework directive for the Community's worker health and safety programme was adopted on 12 June 1989. Five EC directives set minimum requirements for the workplace, design and use of equipment, protective clothing and equipment, handling of heavy loads and the use of visual display units. The VDU directive has implications for voluntary organisations as employers. Special attention is to be paid to agriculture, construction, work at sea and the extractive industries. As part of the European Year of Safety, Hygiene and Health Protection at Work in 1992, the EC has organised training courses for teachers, doctors and workers in some high-risk activities. Studies were made of the health and safety problems in small and medium-sized businesses in order to inform their managers. There were also some pilot actions for the training of such managers.

12.4.2 Research and development

A Community research programme covering, among other areas, health and medical research, spans the period 1990-4. The new feature of this programme is that it includes research instead of just co-ordination of research. The fourth framework programme will cover the period 1994-8.

Over £4 billion (5 billion ecu) has been allocated to the 1990-4 programme of which 2.7 billion is allocated to 1993/4. The six broad areas for funding are

(i)   information technology/enabling technologies;
(ii)   industrial and material technology;
(iii) environment and lifestyles;
(iv)   life sciences and technologies;
(v)   energy; and
(vi)   human capital and mobility (designed to encourage the mobility of young post-graduate researchers in the area of the exact and natural sciences, technologies and economic science)

Health research

The Biomedical and Health Research Programme, BIOMED 1, was approved in September 1991, and aims to improve the efficacy of medical and health R&D by means of the following objectives:

* better co-ordination of R&D activities among member states;
* co-operation within the Community to apply results and pool resources; and
* encouraging basic biomedicine and health research throughout the community.

Technically, the programme covers the development of prevention, care and health systems (with a budget of 27.5 million ecu), health problems and diseases of major socio-economic impact (72 million ecu, of which 25 million is earmarked for AIDS research), human genome analysis (27.5 million ecu), and research on biomedical ethics (4.6 million ecu). Work on AIDS and cancer are continuing but cardiovascular disease has been added, under the theme of environment and lifestyle-related health problems. Research on the development of medical technology continues to be funded with the addition of the application of information technology to medicine. The Commission is also concerned with tropical health problems, with radiation protection and with the ethical problems of human gene analysis.

Projects must involve a minimum of two mutually independent partners in different member states. Austria, Finland, Norway, Sweden, Switzerland and Turkey are also fully involved in the scheme. The funding can be allocated to large companies, small or medium-sized enterprises (SMEs), institutes of higher education and research organisations. For further information contact Gillian Breen, International Section, Medical Research Council, 20 Park Crescent, London W1N 4AL, Tel: 071-636 5422; Fax: 071-436 6179.

12.4.3 Cancer

The 'Europe against Cancer' programme was launched following the European summits in 1985, with the objective of reducing the number of deaths from cancer by 15 per cent by the year 2000. The first action programme, which ran from 1987 to 1989, culminated in the European Cancer Information Year. The second action plan, running from 1990 to 1994, has been given a budget of £35 million (44 million ecu). It concentrates on the fight against tobacco addiction and protection from carcinogenic agents, and deals with screening, nutrition, cancer registration, bone marrow banks, health education, training and research. There is pressure to ban smoking in public places.

UK contacts include John Orr and John Middleton (prevention), Tel: 071-972 4464 and 071-972 4449 respectively and Patience Wilson (treatment), Tel: 071-972 2000, all at the Department of Health.

A 90-minute video of four films on the Commission's programme of action to fight cancer is available on loan from the London office of the European Commission.

12.4.4 AIDS

The Europe against AIDS Programme was launched in 1991 to run for three years. Much of the EC's work on AIDS has involved exchanging information and epidemiological monitoring. There is a jointly funded EC/WHO European Centre for the Epidemiological Monitoring of AIDS in Paris. The EC wants to develop an information exchange in priority areas such as preventive measures aimed at drug addicts (a programme on preventing AIDS in IV drug users is in preparation), care of infected people and health information and education for young people. Community research policy has mainly concentrated on vaccines, treatments, epidemiology and ways of involving health services, particularly in developing countries, to combat AIDS. The EC will now consider research projects in analysis and assessment of requirements for caring, behavioural factors with reference to prevention, the development of methods for assessing preventative measures, analysis of socio-economic consequences and the preparation of forecasts in this field. Internal market implications such as harmonising condoms and HIV self-testing kits are being considered.

The contact for this scheme at the European Commission is Dr Gouvras, Tel: 010 352 430 131. The contact in the UK is Dr Exon at the Department of Health, Tel: 071-972 3218.

12.4.5 Alcohol abuse

The EC is concerned to provide and support European and national organisations in combating alcohol abuse. It will support a wide range of expenditure on public information campaigns and training health workers in preventing alcoholism.

12.4.6 Drug abuse

The EC is concerned with drug abuse as an issue in its own right and also as part of its policies on AIDS (see ss 12.4.4). It has approved the establishment of a European Monitoring Centre for Drugs and Drug Addiction. The Centre's objective is to provide objective, reliable and comparable information on drugs, drug addiction and its consequences at a European level. It will have a legal personality in addition to concentrating on the collection and exchange of information. The budget for measures to combat drug abuse for 1993 is 3,303,000 ecu (£2.6 million). There is EC funding for a wide range of activities (as under 12.4.8) relating to preventing drug abuse and setting up a Community co-ordinating body for combating drug trafficking. The EC will also give funding for the social rehabilitation of drug users. Further details can be obtained from Clare Moriarty at the Department of Health, Tel: 071-972 4170.

12.4.7 Medical cards

Initiatives include a Council resolution on a proposed emergency health card giving relevant personal health details and a proposed Community medical card to replace the E111 form, which entitles travellers to health cover in other member states.

12.4.8 Public health

The EC has allocated 4.8 million ecu (£3.8 million) in 1993 for measures to combat alcohol abuse (see ss 12.4.5) and for the field of public health. This covers a wide range of costs such as studies, meetings, publications, public information campaigns and training related to the prevention of illness. A new item covers pollution of the environment and public health.

12.4.9 Child abuse

The separate budget covering an information campaign to alert the public to the problems of preventing cruelty to children has been discontinued but is included under measures to assist families and for the protection of children, which has a 1993 budget of 1.3 million ecu (£1 million).

12.4.10 Road safety

The Maastricht Treaty has added to the common transport policy the need for 'measures to improve transport safety'. To achieve this, the European Parliament is proposing the establishment of a European Transport Safety Council, an independent advisory body. It also wants the Commission to set up a task force on road safety, to introduce schemes to improve the maintenance and design of vehicles, and to act to influence the behaviour of drivers, for example, backing legislation on drinking and driving, banning drivers using personal stereos, etc.

12.4.11 Disaster relief

The EC has a budget of nearly 5 million ecu (£4 million) in 1993 to provide immediate relief to disaster victims in the Community. For example, rapid aid amounting to £260,000 (325,000 ecu) was given to victims of the Hillsborough football disaster.

12.4.12 European alternative animal experimentation centre

To encourage and promote alternatives to experimentation on animals and promote a dialogue between public authorities and industry and animal welfare organisations, an alternative animal experimentation centre is to be set up. It will also co-ordinate research in the Community, be a centre for information exchange and encourage the development and validation of alternative methods of research at a Community and international level.

12.5 Key publications

EC Research Funding – a guide for applicants, from the London office of the

European Commission, 8 Storey's Gate, London SW1P 3AT, Tel: 071-973 1992; Fax: 071-973 1900

Framework programme for Community research and technological development, EC, published in the Official Journal (date and reference number available from the London office of the European Commission, 8 Storey's Gate, London SW1P 3AT, Tel: 071-973 1992; Fax: 071-973 1900)

Health and Safety at Work – a challenge to Europe, EC Commission, available free from the Commission's information office, 8 Storey's Gate, London, SW1P 3AT, Tel: 071-973 1992; Fax: 071-973 1900

Research and Technological Development Policy, EC Commission, European documentation, available from the Commission's information office, 8 Storey's Gate, London SW1P 3AT, Tel: 071-973 1992; Fax: 071-973 1900

13 *Consumer Interests*

This chapter is aimed mainly at consumer and user groups, women's organisations, consumer co-operatives, trade unions, industry, the poverty lobby and local authorities which help to implement EC consumer protection law. Third world groups should have common cause with consumer organisations, particularly on the Multi-fibre Arrangement, the Common Agricultural Policy (CAP) and safety issues.

13.1 Key Commission department

Consumer Protection Commissioner: Christiane Scrivener (French)
The key department is the Consumer Policy Service.

Director-General: Kaj Barlebo-Larsen (Danish)

Key officials: Peter Prendergast (Irish), director, Tel: 010 32 2 295 8255, secretary: 010 32 2 295 7258. Jean-Marie Courtois (Belgian, speaks English) general consumer questions, relations with the institutions and consumer organisations, Tel: 010 32 2 295 1720. Address: rue Guimard 10, Brussels.

13.2 Extent of Community involvement

The Treaty of Rome mentions consumers only four times, in connection with the CAP and with competition policy. These are arguably the EC policies of most concern to consumers. However, in order to permit a legislative programme for the benefit of consumers, the EC operates a consumer action programme which was published in *A New Impetus for Consumer Protection Policy*.

The Commission would probably be happy to pursue consumer legislation for its own sake. However, the justification for such laws under the Treaty is sometimes disputed by the Council and members of the European Parliament. As with the environment, EC consumer protection measures stand a better chance of being adopted if they remove barriers to trade, such as those which national labelling laws create. Alternatively, they may end monopolies or unfair trading practices, particularly where trade between member states is affected, as in the case of air transport.

13.3 Key people

13.3.1 In Britain

Christopher Kerse, Consumer Affairs Division, Department of Trade and Industry, 10–18 Victoria Street, London SW1H 0NN, Tel: 071-215 3280

Stephen Crampton, Secretary, Consumers in the European Community Group, 24 Tufton Street, London SW1P 3RB, Tel: 071-222 2662. CECG is an umbrella body for 29 UK voluntary and professional organisations with consumer interests. It researches, co-ordinates and represents their views on EC policies and publishes policy papers, a quarterly newsletter and an annual report. A complete publications list is available.

Stephen Locke, Head of Policy, Consumers' Association, 2 Marylebone Road, London NW1 2DX, Tel: 071-486 5544

Eirlys Roberts, Chairman, European Research into Consumer Affairs, 8 Lloyd Square, London WC1X 9BA, Tel: 071-837 2492

Robin Simpson, Deputy Director, National Consumer Council, 20 Grosvenor Gardens, London SW1W 0DH, Tel: 071-730 3469.

Euro-MPs

For an up-to-date list of members of the Environment, Public Health and Consumer Protection Committee, contact the London office of the European Parliament. Current key members are Kenneth Collins (Labour), Chair, 11 Stuarton Park, East Kilbride G74 4LA, Tel: 03552-37282; Dr Caroline Jackson (Conservative), 74 Carlisle Mansions, London SW1P 1HZ, Tel: 071-222 2160 and Pauline Green (Labour), Gibson House, 800 High Road, Tottenham, London N17 0OH, Tel: 081-365 1892. There is also a consumer Inter-Group in the European Parliament (convener: Pauline Green).

13.3.2 In Brussels

James Murray, Director, European Bureau of Consumer Unions (BEUC), 36 Avenue de Tervuren, Box 4, 1040 Brussels, Tel: 010 32 2 735 3110. UK contacts: Consumers' Association, National Consumer Council and Consumers in the European Community Group.

Albrecht Schöne, EUROCOOP (the EC Consumer Co-operatives' Organisation), rue Archimède 17a, 1040 Brussels, Tel: 010 32 2 230 3244. UK contact: Lloyd Wilkinson, Co-operative Union, Holyoake House, Hanover Street, Manchester M60 0AS, Tel: 061-832 4300.

William Lay, Committee of Family Organisations in the European Communities (COFACE), rue de Londres 17, 1050 Brussels, Tel: 010 32 2 511 4179.

Consumers Consultative Council (CCC), BEUC, COFACE and EURO-COOP, along with the European Trades Union Confederation, are represented on the CCC, an advisory body to the Commission. The CCC has been criticised for including producer interests and for being unwieldy in size and underfunded. Consumer organisations have long demanded the creation of an independent European Consumer Council.

13.4 Current EC policies

The term '1992', synonymous with making the Community a properly common market, has dominated the EC's activities concerning consumers. See the Cockfield White Paper, *Completing the Internal Market.*

On the competition level this should benefit consumers by ensuring a wider choice of goods and services, economic growth, increased competition, reduced border formalities, reduced production costs and freer movement of people and capital. It should also mean that it will be quicker to get consumer legislation adopted in future. The Commission's right to make proposals for consumer protection and public health campaigns will be extended. But it could mean drawbacks such as fewer consumer safeguards, more dangerous products, lower standards and, ironically, even less competition because of increased protectionism against non-EC products and increased company mergers within the EC.

There is concern that making VAT rates the same in all member states would be particularly harmful for UK consumers, as it would mean price increases on food, fuel, fares, publications, children's clothing and shoes. Other issues of current interest to the consumer movement are reform of the CAP and subsidiarity.

Rules governing product safety will come into effect by June 1994. Subjects of discussion at present include the marketing and management of timeshare properties and the liability of suppliers of defective services. Another initiative would simplify cross-frontier sales and contracts.

Peter Sutherland chaired a High Level Group on the Operation of the

Single Market, presenting a report in October 1992. This recommended an action programme which would improve the local enforcement of EC legislation and encourage the co-operation of bodies responsible for such enforcement.

13.5 Funding

13.5.1 Consumer interests department

The only EC fund specifically designated for consumers is the small budget at the disposal of the Consumer Policy Service. The budget for 1993 allocates 2.1 million ecu for consumer policy initiatives and consumer redress; 2.4 million ecu for representation; 6 million ecu for consumer information and comparative tests; 1 million ecu for consumer durables; 3.5 million for product safety; and 1 million ecu for food inspection.

In 1993 the Commission will be proposing its Consumer Action Plan for 1993–4, in succession to the 1990–2 plan. This will guide its spending and may include proposals to improve cross-border redress for consumers, to introduce EC-wide consumer guarantees, and to follow up the Sutherland Report.

Seminars are sometimes funded. Seminars can be on any consumer subject as long as they include representatives from the rest of the EC. Research is unlikely to be funded unless it comes within the department's current areas of interest. You can get some idea of these from the consumer programme, but new ideas are always being incorporated. Even if your organisation does not have research expertise, voluntary bodies are in a good position to obtain the views of consumers through membership surveys or discussion groups, which may interest the Commission. Discuss your ideas with the London office of the Commission.

13.6 Key publications

Completing the Internal Market (the Cockfield White Paper), EC, 1985, available from the London office of the European Community, 8 Storey's Gate, London SW1P 3AT, Tel: 071-973 1992; Fax: 071-973 1900

Consumer Policy in the European Community, 1993 background paper (ISEC/B2/93), from the Commission's information office, 8 Storey's Gate, London SW1P 3AT, Tel: 071-973 1992; Fax: 071-973 1900

Consumer Policy in the Single Market (1991), European Documentation, from the Commission's information office, 8 Storey's Gate, London SW1P 3AT, Tel: 071-973 1992; Fax 071-973 1900

Consumers in Europe, Your Rights in the Single European Market, available from CECG, 24 Tufton Street, London SW1P 3RB, Tel: 071-222 2662

INFO-C, quarterly information bulletin from the Consumer Policy Service in Brussels, by J Ring and D Luquister, Tel: 010 32 2 296 5537

A New Impetus for Consumer Protection Policy, EC Commission, 1985, ISBN 92-825-5668-9, available from the Commission's London office, 8 Storey's Gate, London SW1P 3AT, Tel: 071-973 1992; Fax: 071-973 1900

Product Safety and the Single Market, CECG, 24 Tufton Street, London SW1P 3RB, Tel: 071- 222 2662

Three-year action plan of consumer policy in the EEC 1990–92, COM(90) 98 Final, EC, 1990, available from the Commission's information office, 8 Storey's Gate, London SW1P 3AT, Tel: 071-973 1992; Fax: 071-973 1900

14 *Visiting Brussels*

14.1 Visits to Community institutions

Most of the major Community institutions may be visited by interested groups. Visitors must normally meet their own expenses.

14.1.1 The Commission

Initial requests for group visits should be sent in writing to the London office of the European Commission. Visits are normally for half a day only, and consist of an audio-visual show, one lecture and a general discussion. The maximum number for such a group is 80. Usually at least four to five months' notice is required.

14.1.2 European Parliament in Strasbourg or Luxembourg

It is possible to arrange visits to the Parliament, although not all requests can be met, particularly during Parliamentary sessions. Apply in writing to Avis Furness, European Parliament UK Information Office, 2 Queen Anne's Gate, London SW1H 9AA.

14.1.3 Economic and Social Committee

Address: 2 rue Ravenstein, 1000 Brussels, Tel: 010 32 2 519 9011. Half-day visits can be arranged through the office of Mr Vale de Almeida, Press and Information Division, ECS, 2 rue Ravenstein, 1000 Brussels, Tel: 010 32 2 519 9011. No financial assistance is available. The maximum number in groups is 50.

14.1.4 Court of Justice

Address: Kirchberg, 2925 Luxembourg, Tel: 010 352 43031. Enquiries should be made in writing to Mme Stubbe Ludwig, the Information Division, Court of Justice, Kirchberg, 2925 Luxembourg, Tel: 010 352 43031. No financial assistance is available except to people in the legal profession. The maximum number in groups is 35.

14.1.5 European Investment Bank

Address: 100 Boulevard Konrad Adenauer, 2950 Luxembourg, Tel: 010 352 4379/4371. There are limited facilities for visits of groups (normally not more than 50 people) with interests directly related to the bank's activities in financial capital investment projects, for example from industry, banks, public bodies and local authorities. Some university groups pursuing European political or legal studies, economics, etc. may be accepted. No financial assistance is available. At least three months' notice is normally required. Requests should be addressed to the Public Relations/Information Division, 100 Boulevard Konrad Adenauer, 2950 Luxembourg, Tel: 010 352 4379/4371.

14.2 Ill health

Remember at least to obtain the DSS form E111 before you go, if not insurance as well. A Department of Health booklet, *Health Advice for Travellers*, gives details of eligibility for medical treatment abroad and includes form E111. Form E111 explains whether you are entitled to reduced cost health care should it be needed. Payment for hospital, other medical and dental treatment may be partially refunded. Usually about 75 per cent of the amount paid can be reclaimed from the Belgian sickness insurance fund, following instructions on form E111. There is a proposal in the pipeline for a Community medical card to replace the E111.

14.3 Air travel

Flying is the quickest way to get to Brussels. Economy return air fares from London start from about £200. You can save money (about £75) by staying over a Saturday night, but if you have to cancel you may not get your money back. You should be able to get insurance cover for accidents or illness which prevent you travelling. The flight takes about one hour and you need to allow another 45 minutes to get to Brussels central station from the airport. The time in Belgium is normally one hour ahead of that in Britain. Depending on how far away your home base is from the British airport you can fly to Brussels and back in one day.

Passports are still necessary, although checks have been relaxed at borders between member states. Airports have been requested to reorganise their terminals by the end of 1993 so that passengers arriving from other Community countries are not given the same checks as those from outside the EC. Red and green customs channels have been abolished for travellers within the EC but spot checks will continue.

14.4 Staying overnight

You can reduce costs considerably by getting a package deal of hotel and flight inclusive. You are often required to stay at least two nights, but this can work out less altogether than the standard air fare. Even cheaper is a trip by hovercraft and bus, which takes about four hours from Dover or Brussels, or by ferry or jetfoil and train which take about eight and about six hours respectively from London. However, weather problems can hold up the hydrofoil in winter and its timetable may be inconvenient.

14.5 Choosing a hotel

If you do not use a package deal, the Brussels tourist office publishes a guide to hotels (see s 14.9). You can stay in a fair hotel for around £40 a night. The less expensive hotels are much in demand, so book early. Women travelling on their own will want to avoid the area around the Gare du Nord and perhaps the Porte de Namur district.

14.6 Finding your way around

A train leaves the airport for Brussels about every 20 minutes, stopping at Bruxelles-Nord and Bruxelles-Central (Gare Centrale on the metro). You pay your fare (currently 80BFr, just over £1.50) close to the departure point of the train or at stations. If you pay on the train, a single costs 140BFr. The journey takes about 20 minutes. When you get off, it is useful to note the times of appropriate trains back for your return flight. Gare Centrale is close to the Grande Place and its surrounding area of shops and restaurants. The Commission uses several buildings, some of them quite a distance from the Berlaymont, although all departments use the 200, rue de la Loi address. Before you set out, check which building you want.

The best way for visitors to travel around Brussels is by metro, a very efficient under and overground tram system. (A map is available from the Brussels Tourist Office. See s 14.9). Metro stations are marked by a large M in white on a blue background. Tickets for one journey are valid on the metro, trams and buses. Ask for 'un direct'. For several journeys in one day, you can buy a tourist ticket. If you are staying overnight and will be making more than five journeys, or if a colleague is following you to Brussels, it is worth buying a card of 10 tickets. You have to punch them yourself in the machines provided at the entrance. Cards for five rides can be bought on trams and buses, but cost more than if bought at a station.

If you need to travel by taxi, it is best to order one by telephone or to find a taxi rank. The operators have an agreement not to stop when hailed in the street so that fares are picked up in strict rotation. You do not need to give a tip.

Walking in Brussels is pleasant but crossing the street may be hazardous. If there is a pedestrian crossing, you are supposed to cross there and nowhere else, but there is no guarantee that cars will stop for you. By the same token, when red shows on pedestrian lights you are not supposed to cross whether the road is clear or not, but when green shows it does mean there will be no traffic. It is often the signal for a new stream of traffic to come hurtling round the corner – on the right-hand side of the road.

14.7 Making a telephone call

To make a telephone call you need plenty of 5 and 20 franc coins. Some telephones take credit cards and/or telecards which can be purchased from news-stands and bookshops. The international code from Belgium is 00 and the code for Britain is 44. Thereafter the same regional codes apply as you use in the UK, but without the initial 0.

14.8 Food

Restaurants around the Commission building are expensive, though there are some sandwich bars in the area. By arrangement, visitors to the Commission can get a low-cost lunch in the staff canteen. For a meal out in the evening, you can eat well and at a reasonable price in the area around the Grande Place, but be careful to check the menu and prices before you enter because quality and cost vary greatly in this area.

14.9 Key publications

Belgium: Historic Cities and Week-ends, obtainable from the Belgium Tourist Office, rue du Marché-aux-Herbes 61, 1000 Brussels, Tel: 010 32 2 504 0390

Brussels, New Guide and Map, available from Brussels Tourist Office, Hôtel de Ville, Grande Place, 1000 Brussels, Tel: 010 32 2 513 8940

Health Advice for Travellers, Department of Health, available from post offices or telephone 0800 555 777

Hotel Guide, Brussels, available from Brussels Tourist Office, Hôtel de Ville, Grande Place, 1000 Brussels, Tel: 010 32 2 513 8940

Short Breaks in Flanders, obtainable from the Belgium Tourist Office, rue du Marché-aux-Herbes 61, 1000 Brussels, Tel: 010 32 2 504 0390

Index

149